# Thriving
## *in Business and Life*

*by Will Wilkinson and Christopher Harding*

*Thriving*
*in Business and Life*

ISBN-13: 978-1542748728

ISBN-10: 1542748720

Authors of record: Will Wilkinson and Christopher Harding

Copyediting: Becky Badger Harding

Left-Brain/Right-Brain cover illustration: © Copyright: Shai-Halud Stock illustration ID:484459190 - 2015

For more information about this book and its authors, please visit www.thrivinginbusinessandlife.com.

# Praise for *Thriving*

*Thriving* is the type of paradigm-shifting book that only comes along once in a great while. It's a powerful distillation of the authors' personal and professional experiences, offered to us as practical and inspirational fuel for the evolution of our businesses and personal lives.

> ~ Ben Hummell, MA, LMFT, LPC
>    Author, Summoning Genius: A Midlife Guide to
>    Discovering Identity, Purpose, and Meaning

*Thriving* is a book that will profoundly change your life and your business... if you'll let it! The authors take you through the most exciting discoveries of the 20th and 21st century regarding the human brain, and they share transformative techniques to power through the limiting beliefs we may have about our business and ourselves. They even throw-in a few proprietary "life hacks" honed over their many years of transformational work, to get you to where you've always dreamed of going. What a gift to small & medium-sized businesses that can't afford transformation consultants at a time when they need them the most. A revelatory must-read to empower yourself and your people to not just survive but thrive!

> ~ Pauline Ploquin
>    Chief Relationship Officer, Partner, Struck Inc.

Will and Chris have written a very inspirational guideline for achieving personal and professional success. Most importantly, they have lived what they are writing about. A must-read for anyone interested in creating a personal formula for success.

> ~ William A. Guillory, Ph.D.
>    Author, Spirituality in the Workplace

This is a book of practical wisdom by two men who have done their work. Not simply the work of researching and writing this book but the work on themselves that allows them to authentically write about thriving beyond surviving. Whether you are encountering these ideas for the first time or meeting them again, the vivid personal examples and lively writing make this an engaging and at times moving book to read. Their message is clear, easily grasped and designed for immediate application.

~ Joseph D. Friedman
Consultant, Coach and Transformational Educator

*Thriving* offers a path for truly loving life. With powerful tools that help you navigate your personal or professional journey with grace, it's the perfect message at the exact right time.

~ Danielle Lin, C.N.
Host and Creator of The Danielle Lin Show

# Table of Contents

# Dedication

In compiling the chapters for this book, both of us have acknowledged various people for their contributions to our lives. On the pages that immediately follow, however, we want to make special mention of a few key people:

WILL:

I never write alone.

Yes, I may sit alone at a keyboard but every word I write has many signatures on it. I'd have nothing to write if not for those family, friends, and associates who've starred in my stories and supported me to tell them.

Thanks to my mother who taught me to love words and bought me my first book, a treasure I still own. I remember those childhood nights, listening and then reading, enthralled for life by the spells we shared.

Thanks Dad, for inspiring me with the major sea change you made late in life, proving that it's never too late to become the better person we know we can be.

Grandfather, you're woven into these tales, thanks to the passion for life you imparted to me in that one last, long gaze before you passed.

Beverley, my first wife, a superb writer—she's in here. As are Mr. Washburn, my high school English teacher; Bill Bahan—the most entertaining public speaker I've ever enjoyed; the nameless instructor who wrote the words "Made in Japan" on a flip chart in a business seminar thirty years ago and inspired me to excellence; and my wife of 23 years, Tashina, for her unflagging faith in me.

Finally, I dedicate this book to my personal model for thriving: Mother Nature. I live in a forest and my love for trees and streams and wind and rain grows deeper every day.

I recommend that everyone find more time to be in nature to directly experience what thriving feels like.

I hope the abundance in this book illuminates in some modest way how the same thriving is possible for every one of us in our lives and our organizations.

CHRIS:

There are so many people I want to acknowledge and to whom I dedicate this book. I'll start with my parents. I realize more each day how profoundly fortunate I am to have had a mother and father who believed in me and who, despite their own flaws, continued to influence me for good even as an adult.

Hand-in-hand with my parents, my brother, Ralph, has been a friend, mentor, coach, and business associate who has made my life richer and my mind wiser. Also, in ways I'll never be able to properly articulate, my son Jesse and his wife, Erin, and my grandkids, Grace, Sam, and Jonas; and my son Chris and his wife, Michelle; and my son Davey are treasures in my life that continue to bless me with their patience, honesty, and forgiveness. They have been—and continue to be—some of my most significant teachers.

My dedication would be woefully incomplete without acknowledging my Creator. It's impossible to explain how profoundly my life has been molded and my heart remade through the grace of this ever-present Life Force that seems to be unflinchingly committed to my growth and ongoing transformation even when I'm not. Whether in meditation, prayer, dreams, intuition, or through others in my life, it is the Voice of Love that constantly brings me back to my center and the deeper truth of my life. To me, it is this Spirit of Compassion that is at the very heart of thriving.

I also want to thank the numerous influences I've had in my personal and business life. Friends too numerous to mention, each special in their own way, have shared their hearts and souls with me and enriched my life and path. I especially want to acknowledge my friend and mentor Bill Guillory. Much of what I've contributed to this book has come from what he's taught me over the years.

To call out but a few, my concepts regarding diversity, values, responsibility, and empowerment are foundational principles I learned as I worked alongside Bill as a facilitator, coach, consultant, and trainer for 18 years. I can't begin to imagine where I'd be had I not encountered him at a crucial intersection in my life.

For Samantha, who regularly pays me the honor of calling me, "Dad," you continue to amaze me with your own tenacity, drive, and commitment to thrive, even in the face of tremendous odds.

And last, but certainly not least, I want to acknowledge and dedicate this book to my life partners—my ex-wife Becky, with whom I shared over 20 years of marriage; and my current wife Lila, who's been my partner in life for nearly 14 years. Each of them, in their own way, has shown me the depth and beauty of love and partnership. Their own individual gifts and powerful ways of interacting with life have supported me, challenged me, and always led me to be a better man. My deepest thanks to you.

# Foreword

Who are you? Really? It is a question we often answer with our name, which is correct. Yet, there is more to this question. Right?

A few years ago, a good friend, Bob Boylan, author of *What's Your Point?* said to me, "You will be the same person five years from now except for the places you go, the people you meet, the books you read and lastly, but most important . . . the risks you take."

I have found all this to be true—in fact, his words changed me.

Reading this book is a risk. It will change you. It will help you distill the deep, exciting and fulfilling answer to the question, "Who are you?"—a question we answer over a lifetime.

You will discover the following: you have it in you to succeed; you have a vision; you know what matters to you and what really lights you up. This is a "How To" manual that will energize you personally with a doable game plan to truly thrive and help bring your company from "almost there" to "We did it!"

I believe every one of us has a responsibility to leave the world a little better than we found it. The authors, Will and Chris, clearly feel that responsibility. Yet, they are like us, living with the highs and lows of life. Along this roller coaster ride they have each learned something about who they are and gained some remarkable insights. They speak from real experience, having helped countless individuals and companies do just what you want to do—see your dreams come to life. It is their privilege and joy to share what they have experienced. It comes from a place of love.

Recently Dove Soap ran a fascinating campaign where they asked a police sketch artist to stay behind a screen and draw the people sitting on the other side by simply listening to them describe themselves. Then several friends of the person being drawn were invited by the artist to offer their feelings about what made this individual special. Two drawings were created from these conversations.

The sketches of these people were then placed side by side and the individuals were brought back to see them for the first time. In every case, the drawings based on the friends' descriptions depicted a bright, smiling, warm and wonderful person. However, the drawings based on the person's self-description were sadder and less inviting. Why?

Is there some kind of "limiter" inside us that won't allow us to see the good others so easily observe? What would happen if we saw what others see in us? What if we discovered that there is much more inside than we ever imagined? I believe we would change. And it would make us smile. We really are very special and have much to offer each other.

Our decisions in life are made against a backdrop of our foundational values, the character traits that make us who we are. I believe each of us comes with all the values we will need to handle whatever happens in our lives. We may fall in and out of love, have extreme ups and downs, great happiness, tragedies, physical and emotional stress, embarrassing failures and remarkable success. Each event shapes us and helps us see the values that influence our every decision.

You may recall the story of Sully Sullenberger, now captured in the wonderful film, *Sully*. In January of 2009 he was piloting a Boeing 737 over New York City when a flock of geese crossed his path and were sucked into the engines, silencing them. With no power, 155 people on board and 208 seconds ticking away before he either crashed or landed . . . he successfully glided into the Hudson River. Everyone lived. It was indeed a miracle on the Hudson. Some have described Sully as calm under pressure, clear thinking, compassionate, responsible—and the list goes on. Pause for a moment and ask yourself, "What if even one of those values were missing? Is it possible there would have been different outcome?" Yes, it is very possible.

What about us? Do our values matter? Yes. They matter. Our values define us.

I invite you to take a risk and read this book.

To discover who you *really* are. To learn something special about yourself that you did not know was there. To find that you have all the values you need to be successful. To live a life more like you want it to be. To know that you are already making the world a better place because of the special gifts you possess.

And . . . to thrive!

Gary Dixon, President
*The Foundation for a Better Life*

# Introduction

*Every living system on our beloved planet
is an eloquent expression of the universe's astonishing
ability to come into perfect balance;
and to then do what life is meant to do,
to thrive; Thriving is the natural flow of life.*

~ From the Movie, *Thrive*

To thrive or not to thrive, that is our question.

Over decades, we've worked with everyone from Fortune 100 CEOs to parents and retirees, with one intention: how can we help people move from survive to thrive in their careers and in their lives?

Surviving means barely keeping your head above the water; thriving means surfing a wave of success and happiness that's not based on external factors. In fact, the clarity that comes with thriving often transcends our circumstances and leads us to more viable options.

Because the ability to thrive, even in the midst of difficulty, is increasingly important in our world, we recently refined our prospective client pre-qualification formula:

*How can we help individuals and organizations
who are truly committed to doing good in the world?*

The folks who run our local hardware store definitely fit that description. Their customer service is great and the products they stock (expertly managed) keep our community builders and maintenance experts in business.

That's pretty important to the life of our town.

Like so many small business owners, these folks are honest, competent, and caring. Why shouldn't they benefit from the kind of consulting that larger enterprises can afford?

We made a decision to offer our two lifetimes of experience to help good people do good things, for a minimal financial investment. At this point in our lives we can afford to do that and we want to.

9

It's been a smart decision; we work with dedicated, good-hearted people and companies large and small who are ready for an upgrade to the software of their hearts and minds.

Now, in this book, we're bundling together what we've learned and presented for the benefit of all the clients we will never meet . . . the readers whose paths we may never cross.

We hope these materials help you succeed, in direct proportion to the valuable services you are offering.

## WHO ARE WE?

WILL: My wife's voice sounds different on the phone. "Please, come home right away." I drive fast, wondering and worried. As I pull up to the house, I remember she had an appointment with the doctor today.

She is sitting on the couch when I burst through the door. I settle into the living room of our cozy Ashland home. The fireplace is blazing. Our cat is asleep on her lap. She looks peaceful. We lock eyes.

"I have cancer."

Shock. Disbelief. Tears. Shrinking . . .

The next three months are a blur. We somehow find our way through a maze of options, warnings, recommendations, and implications, and, finally, surgery.

Millions of people have spoken or heard those three words, "I have cancer," but that's just statistics until you hear or speak them yourself.

Eight years later, as of this writing, my wife is healthy. And, she's become my hero! The way she engaged fully with her condition and left no stone unturned in taking personal responsibility for her recovery . . . amazing.

To say that she inspires me doesn't do justice to the power of her example. She likes to say, "Cancer is not a death sentence, it's just one word."

What is this teaching me? To be unafraid to face big problems and fully engage with them . . . all the way through.

This attitude saved my wife's life.

It's shown me the meaning of mine: to engage.

Some people believe—I'm one of them—that life tends to bring you what you need just when you need it, to continue growing as a person. This was a perfect example.

It forced me to engage more fully than I ever had. It's difficult, even if you're willing. Now I take that understanding into my work with people, with a lot more empathy and compassion for the very real challenges everyone faces in confronting what's really going on.

Socrates said that "the unexamined life is not worth living." Sometimes we get a gentle nudge, sometimes it's a whack on the head. Whatever it takes, life is too precious to waste on surviving when we could be thriving.

CHRIS: It's January 17, 1994. Martin Luther King Day. Los Angeles, California. I'm in bed, sound asleep. I'm awakened at 4:33 a.m. Something's terribly wrong! The walls are trembling.

So am I. It's an earthquake.

Violent chaos ensues. Pictures fly off my walls. I'm thrown out of bed and crawl to a nearby doorway. It's weaving back and forth wildly.

A transformer explodes on the pole outside my window. I feel my heart stop.

Oh God! I pound my chest in vain, trying to get my heart to start up again. I'm determined, but I'm losing consciousness. My life flashes ·before my eyes . . .

I die.

For nearly ten minutes my heart does not pump. The oxygen drains from my lifeless body. I find myself in a whole other world.

It's amazing, but I'm not done yet. There is so much left to do, family to love, clients to help, a purpose to fulfill.

I make a clear choice and a channel seems to simultaneously open. I know what I must do and with one mighty push, I dive down the channel and back into life, back into my body. My empty lungs gasp for air. My eyes pop open. I'm alive again!

And, I'm still here. Every morning now, I awaken with gratitude and those words resonating in my head: "I'm alive again!"

Questions immediately follow: How will I live today? How will I use this precious life I've been given? Who can I help? Who can I learn from so that I can do an even better job of sharing the gifts of knowledge others have shared with me?

Some days—most days, actually—I do well. I thrive! Some days I don't. I merely survive.

While I'm not particularly fond of those survival days, they always prove instructive. I'm able to examine those patterns of thought and behavior that distracted me off the thriving path to tumble down a less productive and much rockier trail.

That slip-and-recover dynamic is important for me, you too. It happens to us all and it's honest to admit it. I doubt you'd take much of what we write seriously if we pretended we were beyond that. No, we all teach best what we are learning for ourselves.

So, yes, we've stumbled. And, gratefully, we've learned how to recover quickly. We're excited to share how we do that with you.

## OUR BIG WHY

From the moment the two of us met, we knew we would work together. As we got to know each other, we marveled at the similarities in our personal histories.

It seemed like two streams of experience and initiative were merging. So, what would we do with this friendship?

We were on the same career page—in a wiser season of life with an interest to contribute closer to home more of the time, to bring our skills and experience into organizations and families committed to the values we cherish—integrity, open-mindedness, and leadership by example.

CHRIS: In my consulting company, I'd worked primarily with Fortune 100 companies. For two decades, I traveled the world advising, consulting, and training leaders to create and sustain winning corporate cultures through inclusion and leading-edge business strategies.

WILL: I'd worked in the nonprofit sector for over 20 years and more recently developed a private consulting practice, working with individuals and small, charitable organizations.

Both of us were concerned that businesses large and small are facing new challenges in an increasingly unpredictable world. As the stresses of life increase, incremental changes just aren't working. And old approaches aren't working the way they once did.

We both knew that a fundamental change was needed and we found a simple way to map it—moving from survive to thrive.

Years of experience had taught us that the arbitrary line between personal and professional life is blurring and disappearing. We also knew that very few individuals truly understood how to live their values consistently at work and at home.

Obsession in any direction inevitably creates depletion elsewhere and surviving requires compromise.

People do survive for the most part (at least until the stress wears them down), but everyone needs help to learn how to thrive. That's because thriving is a group model, no Lone Ranger or Wonder Woman superheroes are called for.

We realized that now is the perfect opportunity for the two of us to combine forces and launch ourselves into this final chapter in our careers. We're in our sixties and the idea of retiring makes us laugh.

In many ways, we're peaking right now. Except for not being able to dunk any more. Wait, neither of us could *ever* dunk!

Truly, we feel confident that we have more to offer than ever before, two lifetimes of experience, lessons learned, and skills developed. And the humility that comes with failing and improving and understanding what made the difference.

## WHY A BOOK?

Combing through decades of materials, we discovered fundamental principles worth going public with. What better way than . . . a book!

So here it is, this book, plus a comprehensive mentoring/consulting program for individuals and organizations (accessible through our website).

Life has given us both a lifetime of learning opportunities. We've both been mentored by remarkable leaders, and we've gained some measure of wisdom that can't do any good until we share it.

## WHY READ IT?

In our work as media producers and executives and through two decades as executive coaches, leadership consultants, and facilitators, we have discovered, tested, and perfected a range of now- proven techniques unknown to the average person.

Even executives and leaders of high-level organizations aren't conversant in many of these processes.

Why aren't these techniques well known and put to good use?

They're too simple. Simple gets overlooked. But not by us. We like to ask, "What's the quickest, easiest, best way to move from survive to thrive?"

These processes work. So, why aren't they in general practice?

All innovators know the drill. Gandhi said, "First they ignore you, then they laugh at you, then they fight you, then you win."

That all takes time, five to seven years for early adopters to clear trails, then a few more years (at least) before resistance to change wears thin enough that novel ways of succeeding are absorbed into the mainstream.

Meanwhile, anyone who's open to positive change can gain an advantage if they don't put up resistance. They can upgrade from surviving to thriving.

## FROM SURVIVE TO THRIVE

We start with individuals.

Individuals make up organizations. As individuals change, so changes their organization.

You might ask yourself, "Am I surviving or thriving?" How would you know?

When you're thriving, everyone knows it. They feel it when they're with you. You're magnetic. When you're thriving, stress is invigorating. Day-to-day challenges light you up. Your zest for life is contagious.

What about surviving? Stress eats away at you. Fear drives your decision-making processes. Challenges wear you down. Your life force wanes.

All of us have memories of thriving.

We also have routines for surviving. This book explores how to shift gears, change habits, and make everything easier.

## WHAT'S LOVE GOT TO DO WITH IT?

When you're thriving, love becomes your deepest underlying motivation.

Love for life, love for your family, your friends, yourself, your world, your work, your calling, and whoever or whatever you consider to be the source of your being.

We'll get into the science behind this as we proceed, but for now let's clarify that what we refer to as "love" is your most potent ally. Love has significant, positive, and measurable effects on our physiological and psychological states.

And, without a doubt, love *positively* impacts the bottom line!

Love (or vital life energy) is at the heart and core of thriving. Love—when it's properly directed—induces a high-performance state of being.

In this book, you'll discover specific, direct methods for accessing these states and, equally important, you'll learn how to spread the wealth.

**LOOKING FORWARD**

This book provides a map from surviving to thriving, traveling through six segments:

1. Identifying the difference between facts and the stories we tell about them.

2. Detailing our understanding of "vision" and how to create compelling motivators.

3. Growing situational awareness through shedding unconscious (and conscious) prejudices.

4. Assuming responsibility to assemble teams of 100% accountability.

5. Flipping the script of your organization and life.

6. Implementing, summarizing, and focusing on how to integrate and embody habits for thriving.

## THE POWER OF STORY

In our first section, you'll learn the difference between facts and the stories you are telling about those facts, as it applies to your organization and life.

You'll learn how to write a new story. You'll pick up skills to create a thriving context that empowers change and success. You'll consider the impact of unconscious bias and how it undercuts plans, limits thinking, and sabotages even best practices.

## VISION FIRST, RESULTS NOW

Every innovator hopes to develop their own "secret sauce." Here's ours.

We've developed a unique process of visioning that incorporates vital ingredients missing from every other visioning process we've studied.

Our process is designed to provide powerful and lasting motivation.

## EXPANDED AWARENESS

In the next section, we'll introduce you to the cognitive skillsets employed to develop Upstream Perspectives. UPs afford you new insights for formulating accurate assessments to execute strategic course corrections.

You'll learn how to optimize efforts and relationships by traveling in "deep time."

By leveraging the genius of inclusion, you'll heighten personal and organizational intelligence.

## QUANTUM RESPONSIBILITY

In Section Four you'll encounter two paradigm-shifting principles: quantum responsibility and exponential empowerment.

Our clients often tell us that the clarity and reliability generated by applying these two principles and their accompanying practices are huge game-changers.

**FLIPPING THE SCRIPT**

Finally, we'll complete this learning adventure by teaching you a well-honed process we call flipping the script.

You'll learn how to reverse counterproductive trends and initiate a new chapter in your personal life and organization, to access the genius of adaptability, improvisation, and your brain's remarkable ability to make its stories real.

**WHAT'S CALLING YOU?**

What lights you up?

What do you feel called to do? Who do you feel called to be?

These are simple, profound, and seldom-asked questions. Could now be the best time to answer them?

I (Chris) remember asking my father "How will I know what career path to choose." I was 17, about to take my college entrance exams. His answer was clear and simple.

"Just ask yourself what you'd love to do, even if you don't get paid, and make that your vocation."

I thanked him and walked away with a measure of clarity. But I soon returned with another question: "What if I stop loving what I'm doing after a while?"

"Simple," my father answered. "Decide what you'd love  to do next and make that your career path."

My father was teaching me to follow my calling.

Later he told me: "You are going to spend most of your waking hours at your job. Make sure you're spending that precious time and energy doing something that truly matters to you. If you don't," he warned, "your personal life will suffer."

I (Will) was 25 when I enrolled in a three-month training program related to the work I was undertaking in an international education nonprofit organization.

I learned that the CEO, an elderly man I was in awe of, had chosen me to represent the class in graduation ceremonies. During a session break I approached him nervously and told him that I appreciated his vote of confidence.

His response was abrupt. "Good," was all he said.

He inspired me in reverse. His lack of empathy taught me to do the opposite.

I doubt he intended this result, but my mentor was teaching me to be a fully feeling human being.

## NOW IS THE MOMENT

It's not too late to get in touch with what you're passionate about.

Whether it's your job, your avocation, or a family project, what matters is that you find a way to thrive, to love your life, and to love what you're doing.

Many years ago, another one of my (Will's) mentors advised me that if you want to exert an influence you must apply your effort where the influence is needed.

I'm not sure I fully understood that principle at the time but I learned. The shock of my wife's cancer diagnosis forced me to confront my avoidance habits and stay fully present to deal with the challenging details.

You have your own challenges and habits for avoiding them. Think about your latest to-do list. What slipped down to the bottom? What didn't you want to do?

Chris died and returned. Will's wife got cancer and recovered. We've both faced life and death challenges that forced us to engage.

We've learned that *this* is our true calling—to confront survival challenges and leverage them for opportunities to thrive . . . and to help others do exactly the same.

## WHO ARE WE SPEAKING TO?

We have no interest in supporting business-as-usual practices for individuals or organizations lost in self-serving narcissism or consumed by the drive to become successful at the expense of others.

We won't help you fight for a bigger piece of the pie—that's operating from a scarcity model. But we are very interested in helping you make a bigger pie.

Extraordinary times call for extraordinary individuals, organizations, and communities. Are you one of these?

OK. Let's get started.

# PART ONE

## What's Your Story?

*Where we learn
the difference between facts
and the stories we tell about them.*

*What will your new story be?*

# Chapter One:

# The Power of Story

*Doing the same thing over and over again*
*and expecting different results*
*is the definition of insanity.*

~ Albert Einstein

Ed is a plumber. Every day he breaks for lunch with Jack, an electrician he met on the job. Every day Ed opens his lunch bucket and says, "Cheese sandwiches, every day, cheese sandwiches!" After a week of this, Jack can't remain quiet any longer.

"Look, if you're tired of cheese sandwiches, why don't you ask your wife to make you something different for lunch," he asks?

"Wife?" Ed replies. "What wife? I'm not married. I make my own sandwiches!"

## WE ALL MAKE OUR OWN SANDWICHES

It's easy to see Ed's insanity but what about our own? If we're honest, we've all done the same in our own way—repeating a familiar pattern of behavior and acting surprised when it generates the very same outcome, over and over again.

Ed complaining about having to eat the same sandwiches every day, sandwiches *he* is making, seems ridiculous. Why doesn't he just make different sandwiches?

Why don't we change habits we know are hurting us and those closest to us? Why won't we do what we know we need to do at work to make things go more smoothly? Why don't we exercise the way we know we should?

Why is it so hard to adapt, to change direction or take a different approach, even when we don't like where we're heading? Let's find out.

**WHAT'S YOUR STORY?**

Imagination. It's a powerful tool.

All of us have the ability to envision the future. There's another function of our imagination, however, that's constantly running in the background—quietly, almost imperceptibly—the ability to create stories.

All of us are storytellers. It's what we humans do.

It's unconscious. Much of the time, it's also hypnotic. In fact, most of us are hypnotized most of the time, living under the spell of our own stories.

Some say that creating stories is one of only a handful of truly exceptional characteristics that humans possess. Of course, that's a story too because we don't really know if it's true. But it bolsters faith in our exceptionality, doesn't it?

OK, back to *this* story. We may agree that we make up stories but do we realize that we are making up stories *all the time*?

Stories when we get up, stories when we go to work, stories when we interact with our family, stories when we're in the neighborhood, stories while we're driving (especially about other drivers!).

We're constantly creating stories.

Our mind's story-making machine is ceaselessly running behind the scenes in an endless story loop. Different versions of each story repeatedly play out day-by-day, month-by-month as we cast the current people in our life into unresolved roles from our past. Once we become aware and begin to pay attention, it's truly remarkable to witness.

We even tell stories in our sleep. They're called dreams.

It's as if we can't *not* make up stories, as if our brains are *hardwired* for stories. In fact, when we tell or hear stories our brains light up in exactly the same areas they would if what the story is describing was actually happening.

Here's where storytelling gets truly intriguing. Our unconscious mind (which scientists estimate makes roughly 95% of our decisions) doesn't know the difference between something we're imagining and something that's actually happening.

This helps explain why the movie and video game industries do so well. They're selling experiences that seem real to our unconscious minds.

As we'll discuss in more detail in a later chapter, this also explains why sports psychologists train athletes to use their imaginations for visualizing success. The more vividly the high jumper, skier, or free-throw shooter can see themselves performing successfully, the more their body and mind will work together to convert that imagined reality—their story—into a physical result in the 3-D world.

## STORY MORPHING

Let's start at the most fundamental level and learn about the stories you are telling in your life and organization. Is your primary story about surviving or thriving?

We're not asking you to consult the *facts* of your life but to access the *story* you are telling about those facts. If you can grasp the difference between the facts and the story, if you can realize that you are superimposing meaning onto those facts, then you're ready to learn about what we call "story morphing."

Let's begin by examining the story-making process itself.

We all have tremendous natural ability to generate stories. But it's a capability we simply have not been educated to use properly.

The stories we create—including who we are and what role others play in our lives—are scripted from the available content in our personal story bank. Without even thinking about it, we regularly access our personal history, habits, preferences, etc., and then customize those details to create a story.

We'll add a little spice here, underplay some things there, maybe exaggerate others, confer a particular meaning to one aspect, assign a motive to another. This is what we call "story morphing" and most of it is done unconsciously.

You might say, "I never do that! I always say it the way it is! I always tell the truth."

"Whatever you gotta tell yourself," is how one of our friends from Kentucky would respond to those assertions, accentuating her retort with a wink and a knowing smile. We could be more polite. Let's not. Let's call this what it is.

It's B.S. It's self-delusion.

Scientific research has demonstrated this repeatedly. In fact, in one study done at the University of Massachusetts at Amherst, most subjects lied three or four times during a mere ten-minute conversation. These alterations of the truth were often small, seemingly meaningless adjustments depending on the context and who was present. But, just as we've described, each person's stories morphed, based on the circumstance.[1]

We do it. You do it. All of us are doing it, all the time.

Fact is, while you no doubt make a concerted effort to be truthful, truth is subjective. It looks different, seen through the eyes and lives of each individual.

If we were to ask you to describe someone in your life—a family member, a colleague, a friend, or perhaps a person you did not like— the answer you'd provide would be *your* story about that person.

While that may seem obvious enough right now as you read these words, in the moment we can easily forget and assume that *our* experience of a person is "the truth."

No. What's actually happened is that you have unconsciously melded *your* perception of that person with the facts so thoroughly that they have become one and the same to you (and, you may think, to everyone else).

The problem is that they're *not* one and the same.

When we act as if they are, we're deluding ourselves. This means that we limit our perspective and our options dramatically.

Someone else may have an entirely different experience of that person than we do, because they are making up their own story about them (just like we are). They are making their inferences about that person's behavior or choices (just like we did).

## THE DANGER OF COALITIONS

Things get particularly tricky when we attempt to validate the legitimacy (i.e., the "truth") of our story by generating agreement with others. There's a serious flaw to those liaisons because we tend to seek out coalitions with people who we sense will agree with us. We call those people our friends, our allies . . . these are the people we trust.

Whether we realize it or not, building coalitions of agreement like this creates one of our most dangerous vulnerabilities. In the extreme, we can fall under the spell of "mass hypnosis." This is a condition where a number of people share and empower the same misconception or delusion with one another.

Think about all the ways we form agreements with others to strengthen *our* version of reality. How often do we stop and really question why we are doing this?

Suggestion: question "reality" regularly.

What about the poor souls who don't agree with our version of a story?

We can tell ourselves they are wrong, misinformed, or disillusioned. We can assign motives to their choices. We can decide they are not our friends, especially if they disagree with something important to us.

## THE TRUTH CAN HURT

Early in my career, I (Chris) had a manager who I considered to be a real jerk. He got easily stressed out, was often impatient with people, and regularly got red-faced in meetings for reasons that seemed to defy logic.

What's important to notice here is the difference between the facts and my story about the facts.

The facts: He was easily stressed out and impatient, and his face would get red in meetings.

My story about those facts: He is a jerk!

Once I had applied that label to him, he was no longer "one of us." He was the enemy and I commenced to build a coalition of people who agreed with me.

We'd give each other knowing nods during meetings, happy to be accumulating even more evidence to fuel our dehumanizing campaign. Before long we had decided that our manager was not only an obstacle to *our* success, he was also a hindrance to the entire company's well-being.

When I later discovered that his wife was dying an excruciating death from cancer—a horrifying event over which he had no control—the reason for his behavior became clear. Then, instead of treating him with what I had considered to be justified disdain, I began to slow down and spend more quality time with him.

This change in my behavior rankled some of my colleagues. Apparently, I'd done too good a job of convincing them that he was unworthy of our compassion.

It was during a moment when I re-engaged with him as a real human being that he confessed how badly he felt for the way he'd been behaving.

"I'm just so torn," he told me. "I've been taking it out on all of you because I feel like I should be spending every moment with her. But I need this job. I need the health insurance and my paycheck to get her the help she needs. We're drowning in debt from all of her treatments," he shared. "I just don't know what to do."

The tables had turned. Now, with the behind-the-scenes reality glaringly clear, I realized that *I* had been the insensitive jerk.

Over time—and with dedicated effort on both of our parts—we smoothed over some of the wounds I'd inflicted. Only a few months after my turnaround, however, my manager's wife died.

As I witnessed his grief, I took some minor solace in knowing that my change of heart had at least relieved a little of the stress in his life.

It was a hard and painful lesson for sure, but one I've never forgotten.

## WHEN FACTS AREN'T FACTS

You might protest: "Wait a minute, guys, surely there are *some* facts that are . . . well, just FACTS! Not everything is a made-up story!"

And that's true . . . sort of. What we call facts are starting points, the outline for a story. Then we *enlist* those facts to support some story we make up.

We color the facts.

We emphasize some details and ignore others. We don't mean to, not consciously, but it's what the subconscious mind does and it's automatic.

Here's a story that illustrates this phenomenon.

Three men are driving to work early one morning. They stop for a red light and see a naked woman walking across the street. One man is shocked and turns away, offended by the spectacle. The second man is captivated and stares. The third man notices that her eyes are closed.

She's sleep walking!

He gets out of the car, gently nudges her back to wakefulness, offers her the shelter of his jacket and makes sure she gets home safely.

All three men saw the same thing . . . or did they? Where did those different reactions come from? They each made up their own stories based on the "facts" as they morphed them.

Another scenario that illustrates this phenomenon is the breakup story. This could be the breakup of a marriage, a friendship, or a business relationship.

Both parties go through the same factual experiences yet they routinely characterize the other person or party in totally different ways. Each person sees through their own eyes and the lens of their own emotional reality. To them, their story *is* "true" so they can be surprised, disappointed, even outraged when others assign fault contrary to their version of the truth.

The *real* truth is that our reactions to "facts," as we call them, are typically less about the actual facts themselves and more about how we've woven those facts into our own story.

To make this even more intriguing, our story making isn't limited to our personal databases. Movies, the news, TV shows, and social media provide us with plenty of intriguing storylines to choose from. We just copy and paste them into our personal stories.

We spice up our stories . . . without even knowing we're doing that.

But it's not just the stories we tell others that keep us hooked. It's also the conversations we have with ourselves *about* the stories. Here's what we're talking about.

Have you ever noticed how, after some drama has played out between you and someone else, you continue to re-run it over and over again in your head? Only now, you have all the perfect comebacks. And the other person is even more belligerent than you perceived them to be in the actual moment.

Left to our own devices, we can play that type of story loop endlessly, somehow trying to resolve it or have it turn out differently. It's what we do. We fuel the fire, we keep the story alive.

Until we decide to stop it.

## THE VOICES IN OUR HEADS

There's another type of story that can run in our heads as well, one that's even trickier.

When I (Chris) got my first real job in the media communications industry, one of our clients, Dr. Shad Helmstetter, had just produced a program on "Self-Talk." He encouraged those listening to his taped series to pay attention to what they said to themselves, often silently.[2]

As I began to do this, I was shocked to discover the arrows and barbs I'd habitually launched at myself for years. With that type of programming running in the background, how could I possibly hope to overcome the *external* challenges I faced?

Over weeks of conscious effort, I began to reverse this trend by saying, "Cancel," after each negative statement that I made. I'd then replace the self-defeating comment with something productive.

For example, if I caught myself saying, "What an idiot!" after making a mistake, I'd say, "Cancel!"

Then I'd continue with something like, "Wow, that didn't work! But I'm a bright guy. How can I do that differently next time?"

Over time, I trained my subconscious mind to surrender its role as my harshest critic and instead function like a personal mentor. As I experienced the benefits of this transformation, I became less critical and more encouraging of others as well.

## HOW TO POISON A CULTURE

While self-talk impacts our own inner landscape in powerful ways, the tales we publicly weave about others dramatically influence the environment around us.

Such stories can either uplift a culture or decimate it.

When we work with departments or teams that encourage one another through difficulties and cheer each other on, things go well. On the other hand, a common element amongst dysfunctional groups is gossip.

Here are two different storylines, both self-fulfilling prophecies. Which one are you inclined toward? Do you tend to build people up or do you jump on the gossip train? Gossip can be tempting, especially when it's about someone you're not especially fond of.

But here's the deal—gossip is poison!

In fact, there's no quicker way to destroy the morale of a team or company than to allow gossip to run rampant. So, if a toxic culture is your aim, then gossip away to your heart's discontent.

But, if you're looking for a cure—a way to breathe life into a team— there's a simple fix. It's a process called "I've got your back." I (Chris) first learned it in my local church. It  goes like this.

If someone approaches you with a negative story about Jim, for example, you can simply ask, "Have you talked to Jim about this?"

If they say "No," your response is, "You really should go have a conversation with him."

Let's say that their response is "Yes." You can respond with, "Sounds like you need to talk with him some more. And if you need someone to facilitate the conversation, I'm happy to sit down with you both."

Certainly, there *are* times when people need to vent, but too often we allow ourselves or others to poison the well, under the guise of letting off some steam. By following this simple process, though, we create a "No Gossip Zone" around ourselves and we show others they can trust us.

Initially some people may complain when we take this tact, but our recommended response is, "I wouldn't allow someone to talk that way about you either. So, if you're having difficulty with that person, let's figure out how to resolve it productively."

## THE SPELL OF STORY CASTING

We're not implying that stories are bad. Oral traditions and histories have been passed down from every culture. Stories are the way we make sense of our world. They give us a notion of place and purpose, plus a measure of coherence and continuity in what might otherwise seem to be a chaotic and meaningless existence.

Story resides at the heart of every religion and the formation of every nation, at the core of every business and family, and is rooted within the foundation of science.

Yes, even science is a story—a complex, often elegant one—told by scientists based on *their* limited perception of reality as garnered through experimentation and *their* interpretation of facts.

How often do we question our version of the facts? Not nearly enough, we suggest.

Not surprisingly, in our current age, multibillion-dollar industries have sprung up around fascinating stories. Whether it be the movie and television industries, blogs, conspiracy theories, print publishing, public relations, advertising, nightly news, or the video game industry, stories are our primary method of communication, entertainment, and widespread trance induction.

Trance induction? Yes . . . and here's what we mean by that.

## ENTRANCED!

A trance state is simply an induced brain state. There are many induction methods, including television, meditation, chanting, praying, singing, sleep, hypnosis, music, storytelling. The list goes on.

A trance state is induced when cognitive functions such as volition or perception are disabled, enhanced, augmented, or manipulated in some form or fashion and to some degree.

Here's a revelation that will change how you feel about the term "trance." Research indicates that most of us are in some degree of trance state all of the time.[3]

What matters is not *whether* we are in a trance but *what sort* of trance is it? Even more important, are we creating our own trance— casting our own story spell—or are we unconsciously enthralled by the trances of others?

How can we gain more conscious control over our story casting? By learning more about how our brains work.

In the next chapter, we'll do exactly that. Even a brief brain primer can demystify this trance phenomenon enough to help us learn how to write thriving stories, rather than tales of survival.

Informed storytelling can improve our ability to enjoy life and become more successful. We can become more focused and less vulnerable to unwanted influences from others.

## WHAT STORY ARE YOU CREATING?

As a way of grounding the information we've just shared—and as a fun experiment—take a moment right now to make some notes about the story spell you've been casting today, the one you're living in right now.

Ask yourself the following questions:

- *What story am I creating today? (What role have I taken on? What roles have I cast others in?)*

- *Is this story one that I inherited from others? (from family, teachers, friends or perhaps the media?)*

- *Is it leading me to where I want to go?*

- *If I project my current story's course into the future, what are the chances of it ending the way I want it to?*

- *Will this story lead to a solution or keep me mired in a problem?*

To develop more conscious awareness of the power of story, we encourage clients to ask themselves these kinds of questions throughout the day. This is especially helpful when preparing for a critical meeting or pondering an important decision.

This type of story review can become a new habit, one that helps us *choose* the stories we produce, rather than sleep walking through life on autopilot and allowing our narrative to be generated by others or by our own unruly subconscious.

## CHANGING HOW WE SEE CHANGE

In subsequent chapters, we'll guide you through the process of intentionally morphing your stories so that they lead you in the direction *you* want to go.

Here's a key to this: Changing your life starts with changing how you see change itself.

We've all seen those lists that suggest change generates stress; the greater the change the greater the stress. But that's a story too. The process of change, particularly moving from surviving to thriving, can be infused with enthusiasm, hope, excitement, and—believe it or not— it can be wonderfully enjoyable.

We know this because we've learned how to make change and challenges fun for ourselves and for thousands of clients. We've helped individuals, families, teams, departments, and whole companies develop this ability.

The encouraging truth is that when we infuse challenges with a spirit of adventure and fun, our brains perform better, improving our ability to access our natural genius.

And genius, intentionally directed in our lives, makes a difference!

You are a master storyteller. You've been weaving tales all your life. But you've probably also spent years playing roles created and cast by someone else. These roles play into stories that are not who we are and convey little of the unique genius that resides within us.

It's time to take more control over that process.

Imagine telling stories that will take you where you truly want to go, stories that empower you to step into living roles that reveal the ineffable, amazing essence of who you truly are.

Yeah, that kind of story!

It's a story about how to thrive and how to help others do the same!

## CHAPTER ONE INSIGHTS

| SURVIVING | THRIVING |
|---|---|
| Unconscious story morphing—infusing facts with meaning and then acting as if the meaning you impose is factual. | Becoming clear on the facts and deciding what type of meaning you consciously choose to apply, to create a thriving situation. |
| Building self-serving coalitions ·that support only your own position while devaluing and diminishing opposing viewpoints. | Using inclusion to create a more complete understanding so that each and every person involved more fully comprehends other points of view, varied interests, and needs. |
| Ignoring the power of story casting while weaving spells with the stories and gossip that you share about others with whom you work or interact. | Consciously using the power of story and ensuring that the stories you broadcast lead to fair, productive outcomes for you and all involved. |
| Living out stories and roles that diminish your value; telling stories about surviving at the expense of yourself or others. | Living out stories worthy of the beauty of who you are at your core—stories where you thrive and help others to do the same. |

# Chapter Two:

# The Virus of Bias

*All of us show bias when it comes to
what information we take in.
We typically focus on anything
that agrees with the outcome we want.*

~Noreena Hertz

It's decades ago. Alan is a shoe salesman for a U.S. company expanding overseas. His first international sales trip is to rural Africa. He hasn't been on the ground for more than a few hours when he cables headquarters: "Am returning immediately. No market here. So few people wear shoes."

Meanwhile, his colleague Jerry has landed in a different part of Africa. He too sends a cable: "Send samples of everything we've got. Terrific market here. So few people wear shoes."

## A TALE OF TWO STORIES

Same facts, different stories.

Two people saw the world through two very different lenses. This is not an anomaly; it's the way we all experience "the truth." We tell stories about the facts.

As we've just explored, sometimes (if not most of the time) the stories we create are substantially fictional, in spite of our believing that we're telling the whole truth and nothing but the truth.

There is one particularly malignant type of story—it's in a class all its own—that can spread throughout our organizations, societies, and families like a virus.

We refer to these types of contagious stories as "implicit bias."

Everyone has biases. Bias is a perspective, an angle, or a viewpoint. It's a slice of reality, a part of the picture, not the whole thing. Biases show up everywhere a human brain is engaged because it's how the brain works.

Biases are generated as our brains create thinking shortcuts, based on how we've lived and learned and interpreted the patterns in our lives. These shortcuts are meant to enhance efficiency and while it's normal to have them, they can limit our ability to develop innovative solutions.

## PRECONCEPTIONS

The term "implicit bias" was coined by social psychologists to describe a specific type of bias. It refers to our propensity as humans to hold unconscious and unquestioned preconceptions about people who are not part of our group, as if those assumptions were unequivocally true.

Implicit bias often leads to favoritism, prejudice or, in extreme cases, outright bigotry. But let's be clear: everyone is vulnerable to this pernicious virus because it's rooted in unconscious memes installed in our social programming. This programming is regularly reinforced through our social interactions, the media, family, and numerous other mechanisms that are employed in a world that frequently relies upon widespread compliance.

It's helpful that the brain defaults to biases as a shortcut to speed up our ability to make the most effective decisions, but unconscious or implicit bias contributes to systemic problems in organizations and families.

As one executive at a Fortune 100 company recently admitted to me (Chris), "Unconscious bias has become a significant barrier to our ability to effectively solve the complex challenges we now face."

Some organizations have gone so far as to label the brain's shortcut process the "Virus of Bias," because beliefs embedded in biases can spread quickly throughout an organization below the level of conscious awareness, just like a virus.

Over the last decade, a science studying implicit bias has developed, leading to significant leaps forward. For example, Harvard created their now famous "Implicit Association Test" (IAT) that measures the impact underlying cultural and societal biases have on the way we act toward those we consider to be different. Differences explored in the study include gender, race, generation, economic status, height, weight, etc.[1]

One surprising revelation from IAT test results is that every participant discovers how their decisions are driven far more profoundly by imbedded social biases than they imagined. This is particularly jarring when individuals realize they are even acting out biases about themselves.

In our work with organizations, we have witnessed how implicit bias— when active and left unchecked—can produce a dangerous malignant effect that becomes extremely difficult to eradicate. Some companies experience what we term "bias cycles," sabotaging, self- reinforcing cycles of implicit biases (usually unconscious) that contribute to conflict, disengagement, and underperformance for various groups.

When the virus of bias is activated, it invariably develops a divisive "us vs. them" dynamic. This inhibits the ability of those involved to consider and implement solutions beyond the limited views that arise from their personal implicit biases.

What can we do about this? How can we stop implicit bias from spreading like a virus and installing bias cycles in our organization or life?

## UNDERSTANDING HOW IT ALL BEGAN

As we've just described, we all have biases, most of which are unconscious, operating just below the surface as "assumed truths."

Much of this programming occurred when we were young and our brains were biologically primed for immersive learning. Until the age of eight, children's brains are functioning much of the time in the super-receptive theta-wave and alpha-wave states.

Theta-wave and alpha-wave states lend themselves particularly well to experiencing an imaginary world as if it were real. In these states, the logic circuits of the neo-frontal cortex are largely put on hold. It's also important to note that in younger brains, these logic functions are not yet fully developed.

While in this highly receptive age-range, a child's brain is more active than at any other time in life. Almost everything a young child sees, feels, touches, and tastes is recorded unfiltered, directly onto the brain's hard drive (the hippocampus).

Does that trance-like state of mind—where we absorb information almost without thinking—sound familiar? It's the same state of mind we inhabit while watching a movie or television, listening to a powerful storyteller or speaker, or playing a video game.

While in the theta-brain-wave and alpha-brain-wave states we are highly receptive to any ideas and beliefs we are exposed to, especially those infused with intense emotions. Such highly charged experiences are immediately cataloged into our brain's memory bank in a priority position.

The reason this happens directly addresses our theme.

Experiences that have a strong emotional charge (anger, fear, joy, pleasure) are recorded and assigned special significance in the brain when they seem highly relevant to our surviving or our thriving.

Later, as the young adult brain starts ridding itself of what it deems to be unnecessary information, the more highly charged data is kept and assumes a place of prominence in regard to how future decisions will be made.

We mentioned the hippocampus. This is the brain's hard drive, that part of the brain where long-term memories (especially the highly charged ones), were recorded when we were young.

What messages—verbal, visual, and implied—did you receive from your family, your neighborhood, and the media when you were young?

The amygdala, which is positioned right next to the hippocampus, is the survival part of the brain. It triggers the fight, flight, freeze, or faint responses that we react to when we perceive danger.

Is there any significance to their physical proximity?

From a biological point of view, it's no accident. Proximity allows for the most rapid communication and response between our highly charged memory files and the part of the brain designed to quickly divert us from danger's path.

When triggered, highly charged memories and data embedded over our lifetime send priority level signals to the amygdala, alerting us to what we should avoid and who not to trust.

For instance, let's say you were chased by a dog when you were six. It was scary and your brain recorded that intense memory. Now, 30 years later, whenever you see a dog loose on the street you feel a stab of fear and quickly cross the road.

It doesn't matter whether the dog seems threatening or not; your amygdala doesn't differentiate. This is a dog. A dog was dangerous before. It could be dangerous now.

You get your instructions: take preventative action now!

Who and what are the triggers your brain encoded, perhaps years ago, ones that may have been fully necessary then that are still eliciting reactions now, years later, and influencing the decisions you make without you really knowing why?

## BRAIN BLINDNESS

Hand-in-hand with beliefs about who or what to avoid, those highly charged memories influence who you decide has the greatest value to you. It's an ingenious system and it applies to all of us. As mentioned, our brains function in hyper-learning mode during early life.

Young brains take in and record anything and everything they experience. They encode critical memories of perceived threats and potential allies with emotional charges that assign them a permanent priority position in our circuitry.

This early programming continues to affect us throughout life and here's the problem: sometimes (often) that programming is wrong.

Information that may have been highly useful for years, decades, centuries or even millennia, can become irrelevant, even stupendously wrong, especially during periods of rapid change.

According to Manfred Zimmermann in *The Neurophysiology of Sensory Systems*:[2]

- We are bombarded with over 4 *billion* bits of information per second.

- Our conscious mind is only able to process approximately between 400 and 700 *million* bits of information per second.

- That means that most information enters without processing.

- The information we do process and utilize has an essential bias.

- We sort for information that confirms our current reality.

His last point is especially noteworthy. If we sort incoming data to confirm our current reality but our current reality is problematic and needs changing (and when is it not?), we're in trouble.

This fundamental conflict describes what resides at the heart of "brain blindness," a phenomenon generated by the brain's reticular activating system and its habit of focusing on and sorting for what it expects to be true.

Here's a simple example that we'll all be able to relate to.

Let's say you're looking for your car keys. They're lying in plain site on the kitchen counter. But you don't believe they're there because you never put them there.

So, you walk by the counter several times. Your eyes scan the surface and send a picture to your brain of those keys sitting on the counter.

They're right there!

Here's the conflict: your brain is filtering that data out because it doesn't confirm your existing bias (I never put my keys on the counter). Then your spouse walks over and plucks the keys off the counter and laughs. "They're right here!"

I (Will) have a nagging memory like that from childhood. My Dad used to ask for help with various carpentry jobs around the house. He had no patience if I didn't help the way he wanted me to so I developed anxiety about working with him.

He'd ask me to go into the garage to find nails on the workbench. I can still remember the sinking feeling I'd get when he asked, because I knew that I wouldn't be able to find those nails.

And I couldn't.

Search as I might, no nails. But I knew that when I returned empty-handed Dad would snort with disdain, march into the garage, and find the nails right where he said they would be.

There they were, right where I looked . . . seeing nothing!

My problem was the conviction, fear, programming, that I wouldn't be able to find what he asked me to find. Sure enough, my brain cooperated and filtered out the visual of the nails sitting there.

## FACE-TO-FACE WITH BIAS

That's brain blindness and it means, among other things, that we may be surrounded by talents and capacities we simply fail to see—in others and in ourselves.

We may even unconsciously project troublesome motives onto someone that our programming has told us can't be trusted.

I (Chris) was stunned on one occasion to experience just how automatic such programming can be. Though I'd grown up in a neighborhood with friends of varied racial and ethnic backgrounds, my exposure to the implicit bias woven into our media clearly had its effect on me as well, as I humbly discovered one evening.

Picture this. I am returning to the airport after delivering a workshop on implicit bias. I'm exhausted but gratified at how well it went. Before turning onto the expressway and heading for the airport, I pull into a convenience store to get directions.

I turn off the car. A vehicle pulls alongside me in the parking lot. Out of the corner of my eye I notice the driver. He's a young African American man. There's nothing remotely threatening about him . . . not to my conscious mind at least. He could've been one of my friends in another setting.

But my unconscious mind is accessing another database and—before I can even think about it—my left index finger hits the lock button on the car door. Author Malcolm Gladwell calls this phenomenon the "Blink" response.[3]

I'm shocked at my reaction. I look over at the young man in the other car and shrug my shoulders, with an embarrassed expression on my face. He responds by quickly locking his doors and then looks back at me in mock fear.

We both break out laughing.

We get out of our cars and greet each other. I apologize and tell him exactly what happened. I also explain the irony of my having just come from a conference on implicit bias. "Welcome to my world," he says. "This happens to me all the time."

After sharing a meaningful conversation about the impact of our biases, my newfound friend gives me directions to the airport and we shake hands. We even do a quick "guy hug" before I thank him and get back in my car.

"Amazing!" I think to myself as I drive away. The programming of implicit bias runs *so* deep—even in me—and I deliver programs on it!

On the other side of the coin, we may be assuming only the best about other people—people we have unconsciously labeled trustworthy or competent. This phenomenon is known as the "halo effect" and it explains a "teacher's pet," or a manager who gets more face time with the boss, or a sibling allowed to bend the rules when we can't.

## BREAKING THE BIAS CYCLE

Why do these things happen? Clearly, they're not fair. No, they're not, but they happen all the time in both directions.

But here's the good news. . . we *can* break the bias cycle.

We can become conscious of our unconscious biases that drive habitual behaviors, specific actions, and everyday decisions. It starts with owning our own biased-based situations, and being *truly* interested in changing them.

Then we can deliberately create environments where biases—ours and others—can be openly questioned, set aside or changed, in favor of a less delusional reality.

For example, some of our clients now designate a person to serve as a "bias monitor" in meetings where important decisions are being made about hiring or an employee's career path. The individual who takes on this rotating role, listens to ensure that unconscious biases aren't influencing the group's decision-making process.

The following list provides some additional techniques that many of our clients now utilize to eradicate the virus of bias from their cultures and their decision-making processes.

47

## SEVEN STEPS FOR MITIGATING UNCONSCIOUS BIAS

1. Remember that we are all vulnerable to the Virus of Bias.

2. Regularly question your assumptions and stories about other people and situations.

3. Stand upstream and follow the ripple effect of how such assumptions or stories could play out if you continued as is.

4. Purposefully generate a new more productive story that casts people in a more powerful light.

5. Create an environment where it's safe to raise the question about how biases might have entered into our thinking.

6. Consciously replace stereotypes when you discover them in your thinking with examples that run counter to those biased ideas.

7. Create a rotating role of "bias monitor" during meetings and key decision-making processes so that at least one person is able to identify and call to the group's attention, potential biases that may have slipped into the group's thinking.

From this brief tour examining how our brains function and how our programming influences us, we can begin to see how these shortcut systems—helpful as they were designed to be for our survival—could truly use a software upgrade.

How about an upgrade from surviving to thriving? That's exactly what we'll begin developing in the next chapter.

Programming is one thing; values are another. We'll help you identify and more fully understand how to increase the power of your foundational values and the impact they have on the stories you tell and live out in your day-to-day life.

## CHAPTER TWO INSIGHTS

| SURVIVING | THRIVING |
|---|---|
| Ignoring your vulnerability to biases as if you were somehow immune. Dismissing suggestions that you may be acting on a bias. | Being consciously aware of your own vulnerability to biases and inviting others to let you know if they think your actions may be based on a bias. |
| Allowing an "amygdala hijack" to run the show while avoiding or refusing help from others who seek to help you return to a healthier state of mind and heart. | Maintaining an awareness of times when you experience an "amygdala hijack" and asking for appropriate help to return to a more balanced, full-brained, open-hearted approach. |
| Allowing brain blindness to prevent you from fully seeing people's talents, capabilities, or valid points of view. | Seeking input from others to help you more fully see and understand your own blind spots and how they're getting in the way. |
| Creating stories that reinforce limitations and support an "us" vs. them" mentality. | Creating stories intentionally and openly that challenge you to be aware of biases and the divisive dynamics they create. |

# Chapter Three:

# Foundational Values

*When your values are clear to you,*
*making decisions becomes easier.*

~Roy Disney

Lori is climbing her own carefully crafted career ladder. She's intentionally made choices that have allowed her the opportunity to gain more experience and connect with the type of people she knows can help her progress in the fast-paced entertainment industry. In the process, she's moved hundreds of miles away from her family and friends.

It's not the business itself that's driving her. Instead, it's what the access to that world can enable her to do—tell stories that matter, stories of the heart, stories that inspire people to do good in their world.

That's why, when her volunteer work at a local homeless shelter connects her with three young kids who are about to be separated by the foster care system, she puts her career on hold to take them into her home as if they were her own. She doesn't think twice. She doesn't need to. The choice is crystal clear.

To those who don't understand Lori's foundational values, her decision looks totally off-track—or utterly crazy! Why would she do this, just when her career was taking off?

What they don't understand is that her deeper underlying values had never been about career—they had always been about helping the vulnerable, those who had no one else looking out for them.

Her career in the entertainment industry provided a powerful avenue for Lori to realize the values that drove her choices and shaped her life story.

The very values that had compelled her into the role she was now taking on, to be a foster mom to three challenging young kids.

This choice didn't require her to sacrifice her career; it just put it in perspective. It remained important, but she had also found her true calling—helping the less fortunate.

## WHAT DO YOU TRULY VALUE?

Many of us have done exercises where we're asked to list our deepest or innermost values. Words like family, freedom, integrity, truth, love, compassion, creativity, equality, fairness, family, and other noble descriptors often make their way onto our list.

There is often a vague sense of cognitive dissonance that arises during such exercises. Why? Because our *stated* values are very often at conflict with our *lived* values.

For instance, this would have been true for Lori had she become aware of those kids and done nothing about it (because she was too busy with her career).

The types of aspirational values people often list are not insincere. They *are*, however, often a form of wishful thinking. Such ideals may truly come from their heart; they are *stated* values. But they aren't being fully lived yet. This produces conflict and compromise.

Or, the values listed may be "borrowed values," ones we were taught to aspire to, values we were told that we *should* have.

So, what are your current—or as we call them—your "lived" values?

This is not a trick question, and the answer is simple. Just look at this current week. How and where are you spending your time? Doing what?

"That's not fair!" some clients complain when we ask this question. "I have to work to support my family!"

OK. So, who said working was not an appropriate value? Who said pursuing an exciting career was somehow less noble than a seemingly more generous activity?

There's the conflict.

It exists between what you *are* doing and how you *feel* about it (in other words, what you think you *should* be doing). That's a core conflict in survival mode and it's due to misaligned values.

Thriving is resonance, where you are living your deepest values, your decisions are clear, and your actions are not in conflict with your core beliefs.

## GETTING CLEAR ON WHERE YOU STAND

There are times in life when circumstances seriously challenge our ideals and values.

A young couple with strong professional aspirations and a passion for their line of work may struggle to find time for nurturing their relationship. Often the relationship suffers and may even be sacrificed.

Or, they may try to nurture the relationship, at a cost to their career paths. Resentment can follow, as one or both of them may feel they have given up their dreams for someone else. That's what happens if their choices were based on borrowed values, if they did what they *thought* they *should* do.

How do you address what seems like an inevitable conflict, not just between relationship and career? There seem to be so many compromises to make just to live.

To help us get a handle on such dilemmas, we're going to walk you through an exercise.

Take a sheet of paper and divide it in half with a vertical line down the middle. On the left-hand side, write down how you spend your time during the week, doing what for whom. Next to each activity, total the number of hours each week you spend on those activities.

On the right-hand side, write down what you want, wish, or currently feel your foundational values are. Then list the number of hours each week you spend involved in activities that engage those values.

This visual helps you see if your values are aligned with how you spend your time. If you want to get even more detailed, total the hours from both columns and then determine the percentage of total time you spend on each one.

Now, if you find that you are spending an ample amount of your week engaged in activities that further or model your values, go ahead and high-five yourself. Well done!

If, on the other hand, you find that too much of your time is engaged in activities that are not aligned with your values, there are six steps to realign your life with your values. As we walk clients through these steps they often report that taking action on this process restores hope in their ability to truly be in charge of the important aspects of their life.

## SEVEN STEPS TO REALIGNMENT

1. Examine your values list on the right-hand side of the paper. Are those truly your values or are they ones you borrowed from someone else—parents, school, church, friends, society? If so, replace them with your own, the values that light you up.

2. Don't panic if you discover that some of your current lived values seem to be out of harmony. Some values—or their level of importance in our lives—change over time, as we enter different seasons of our life.

3. Look at your activities on the left-hand side of the paper and ask yourself the same question. Which of these activities are you

doing, especially if they're at the expense of your values, because of outside pressure or some notion of what you should do?

4. Imagine yourself nearing the end of your life. Set the stage for this visualization. Who's there? Where are you? Who and what are you going to miss the most? With whom or doing what do you wish you'd spent more time?

5. Now, taking your realizations into account, have another look at your lists. What needs rearranging? Where do you need to make changes to live your values so that you will be at peace when that day comes (and as you end each and every day until that time)?

6. Look at the activities on the left-hand side of your page and draw connecting lines from your activities to any values from the right-hand side that you could consciously and intentionally infuse into those activities.

7. Or, working from right to left, draw a line from your various values to any of your listed activities where those values could serve to enhance the quality of your activities and experiences.

## MOVING TO COGNITIVE RESONANCE

As we take this step of creating more coherence in our lives— between our values and how we spend our time—beware of a mistake that many of us make: We assume that circumstances have the power to determine whether we can or cannot live out our values.

That false dichotomy sets us up for inevitable inner conflict and compromise.

The truth is that circumstances can shape how and with whom our values are lived out, but they don't determine *if* we model and demonstrate them.

For example, if family is high on my list of values and I have a busy career, I could share how my day went with my spouse or partner, my friends, and to some extent—depending on their age—with my kids.

I could invite my spouse to meet me at work for lunch. I could take the kids in on Saturday and show them what I do so they know where I spend my time when I'm not with them.

If I must work late or travel, I could make sure to communicate that fact with family or friends, even with a one-line text. That simple act conveys more than the obvious details. It's a values-based communication that lets them know that I'm thinking of them.

When you *are* with the people who matter in your life, are you *really* with them? Or are you still at work or in some other activity in your head?

Learning to be fully present in the here and now is a critical part of infusing our values into every activity. The same principle applies with your colleagues, friends, or direct reports.

You don't have to wait for special occasions to live your values. If compassion is one of them, you can be compassionate with everyone you encounter, not just those closest to you. If transparency is important to you, create appropriate transparency in every situation.

Integrating your deeper values into all the activities of your life creates coherence. It creates continuity and generates authenticity that is felt by everyone around you.

Living a values-driven life allows you to be consistently who you truly are—and it dissolves the type of duplicity that can occur when you are out of step with your own deeper self.

## A VALUES-DRIVEN LIFE

Once we are clear on what truly matters to us—what we genuinely value the most—we can begin to shape our story accordingly. Our values can redefine the roles we play in our own story and the roles we take on in the stories of others.

I (Chris) was on a flight from New York to Los Angeles a few years back. I had been upgraded to first class and happened to be sitting next to a television and film actress.

We struck up a conversation and she shared that she felt imprisoned by her newfound celebrity. "I can't even go to the corner market anymore without feeling conspicuous," she admitted. "I almost always wear a ball cap and sunglasses so no one will recognize me."

She confessed that this was contrary to her values and how she wanted to show up in the world. "I love people," she said sadly. "Now I feel like a recluse even when I'm surrounded by people."

I asked if she was game for a little experiment over the next two weeks. Her eyes lit up. "Maybe," she said with a tentative smile.

I challenged her to choose times during the coming two weeks when she would go to the store or run other errands without a disguise.

"When you go out," I suggested, "take an intention of spreading the love you feel in your heart for people. Smile at the cashier in the convenience store. Make eye contact and nod. Say hi to someone you pass on the sidewalk. Ask the grocer who always helps you in the market how he's doing."

"You're on!" the young actress nearly shouted.

"Good," I told her. "In two weeks, we're going to sit down for lunch at your favorite neighborhood café and you're going to tell me just how many lives you lit up over the last two weeks."

We met in a small restaurant in the San Fernando Valley a few weeks later. She was beaming and told me stories of all the people she'd encountered and what had happened.

"It's amazing!" she said, her eyes gleaming. She searched for the right words to express her new insight and then she grabbed my arm as a way to ground her thoughts.

"I'm realizing that because of my situation and the way I've been blessed, I can be even more of the person I always wanted to be—someone who can spread joy and hope and love just by showing that I care, in small, simple ways."

**YOUR LIFELINE**

As you contemplate infusing the activities in your life more fully and consciously with the values that truly matter to you, there's a brief experiment we invite you to undertake. It's one that my (Chris) late cousin, Trapper Woods, and our mutual friend Bill Guillory devised for just this purpose. It's a process that was used as an opening exercise in a Work-Life Balance workshop based on their book, *Tick-Tock, Who Broke the Clock?*[1]

On a blank piece of paper draw a horizontal line like the one below.

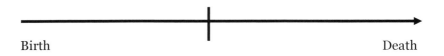

Birth                                                                          Death

We call this your life line. Mark on the line where you think you are in the span between birth and death.

On the "birth-side" of the sheet make note of some of the key experiences and feelings you've had that have shaped or defined your life.

On the "death-side" of the sheet make note of the experiences and feelings you want to make sure you have before you exit your life.

Next, look at the values list you created earlier. Then—next to the future moments, feelings, and experiences you've listed on your life line—record the values you'll infuse into each experience to ensure that you live in harmony with your deeper desires.

If you sometimes find yourself stymied by two competing values on your list, you might consider prioritizing your values to create more clarity. A simple process we use to help clients accomplish this involves our going through their values list with them, comparing two values at a time. But you can do this for yourself.

For example, let's say that two of the values on your list are "freedom" and "professional growth."

The question you might ask yourself is, "If I had to give up some personal freedom to advance my professional growth, would I?" If the answer is "no," then clearly freedom ranks higher on the list. If the answer is, "yes," then professional growth ranks higher.

Some people prefer to go through their entire list this way, comparing one value to another to establish each value's overall ranking. Doing so can create more clarity and provide insight as to the relative importance each value currently has in your life. Remember, your priorities may change over time, but the more clear you become on what really matters to you, the easier it is for you to make key decisions that truly align with your foundational values.

Your values are not mere concepts. They are unique, personal characteristics that you can fill your life with—every day, hour, and moment.

Becoming conscious of your values and intentionally embedding them in your daily routine ensures that you live an authentic life, where circumstances no longer determine the quality of your life. Instead, your true nature will shine brightly into every situation.

We hope you can see the simplicity in this concept. It's not difficult to live a meaningful life, without compromise. It just takes identifying your core values and then living them in both the ordinary and extraordinary moments of your day-to-day existence.

Next, we'll give you a way of doing this immediately and a secret for how you can sustainably live your values as the new normal in your life and career.

Thriving is natural—just look at nature. So much of this work is about returning to a state of being that we already sense is the most practical and enjoyable way to live.

## CHAPTER THREE INSIGHTS

| SURVIVING | THRIVING |
| --- | --- |
| Living life based on borrowed values and what you believe you *should* do. | Becoming clear on what truly matters to you and what truly lights you up. |
| Experiencing cognitive dissonance between your daily activities and your stated values. | Experiencing true cognitive resonance between your daily activities and stated values. |
| Allowing your circumstances to determine how, if, and to what extent you live your values. | Infusing your values into everything you do, no matter what the circumstances may be. |
| Living your life focused on past accomplishments while losing track of where your values fit into the picture. | Looking into the future and becoming clear on what you want and how your values can be infused into your life to ensure that you live with few, if any, regrets. |

# PART TWO

## Vision First—Results Now!

*Where we discover
the primary missing ingredient
in strategic thinking,
discovering how to leverage
our imaginations
to create the results we want,
and experience those rewards
right now.*

# Chapter Four:

# Vision First

*I can teach anybody how to get*
*what they want out of life.*
*The problem is that I can't find anybody*
*who can tell me what they want.*

~Mark Twain

Two young brothers raided the fridge. Brian found a cherry pie, at least the last two pieces of a cherry pie. He offered the plate to Wayne who took the bigger piece.

Brian hesitated for a moment, then said, "You know, when you have first choice it's polite to take the smaller piece."

His brother paused mid-bite. "Really?" he replied, thought for a moment, then added, "So, are you saying that if I'd offered the pie to you that you would have taken the smaller piece?"

"Absolutely," Wayne replied.

Brian resumed eating, chuckled, and said, "Well, what's the problem? You got what you wanted!"

**FINDING CLARITY**

What *do* we want? Do we even know?

There's a saying "Live to fight another day." Doesn't sound very appealing! But it's what surviving is all about.

These two guys wanted different things and that led to conflict, at least for one of them. So, how do we *all* get what we want?

The answer for that has to start with each individual finding clarity about what they personally want. It's rarely simple. In this story, Wayne was clear. He wanted the big piece of pie and he took it. Brian wanted the process of choosing to be fair. How do we solve that?

We go to a different level: vision.

Obviously, we want our problems to go away and solutions to appear, but how? By referencing a vision.

Knowing what we want requires having a clear vision—a vision that's aligned with our deeper values.

Without vision, we doom ourselves to the everyday struggle for survival. We may become highly skilled at problem solving and solution creation but that's not what thriving is about.

Thriving is a state of mind. Thriving develops behaviors that create success and fulfillment far beyond the struggle to survive. Thriving gets us out of bed on dark mornings, thrilled with the day ahead of us. Thriving turns challenges into opportunities and constantly renews our sense of aliveness.

I (Chris) had the good fortune to work with Professor Stephen Hawking and his team a few years back. Our goal was to assist him in creating visual metaphors that would illustrate some of his more complex theories about the universe. He wanted to create a means for everyday people to better grasp the multi-dimensional concepts he saw so clearly in his mind.

I often referred to myself as the "crash- test dummy" for the project. If I could understand the concept, our metaphor was working and other people would understand it too.

What was remarkable to me throughout this process was Professor Hawking's keen sense of vision and clarity. He knew exactly what he wanted and he was very clear about what didn't fit.

Because communication for him is so challenging and hard won, and every moment of life so precious due his battle with ALS, Hawking had learned to condense his requests and pertinent information into beautifully concise sentences.

I remember one occasion when he became concerned about something. He got my attention by practically boring a hole in my head with an intense stare.

When I stepped over next to him to see what he wanted to tell me, he smiled in appreciation. He then used his one working hand to arduously craft a short but precise sentence on his one-letter-at-a-time, mouse-controlled keyboard.

When he was ready, Professor Hawking leaned toward me to ensure we had eye-to-eye contact before pushing the "Enter" key, which would trigger the voice simulator to read what he'd typed in. This was his way of humanizing the synthetic sounding communication. Once we had eye contact, he pressed the button.

"You are off-track. Please stay on topic," the voice simulator stated. I nodded in recognition. I knew he was right and he could see that I got it.

This made Hawking smile again. Message delivered.

Professor Hawking couldn't afford to get off course. Whose idea won, was of no importance to him—only that it be in alignment with his vision. He communicated that in a handful of words.

That's the power of clarity.

## THRIVING BEGINS WITH VISION

Vision comes first.

We're not talking about the standard vision statement that many companies and individuals generate and file. We're talking about a compelling, embodied vision that we remain conscious of throughout the day.

There's a widely-held belief that people prefer the devil they know to the devil they don't know. This explains why we settle for lousy situations.

We might think, "Things may be bad but if I tried something new it could get even worse." That's survival thinking.

## PREVENT DEFENSE

In sports this sometimes shows up as "prevent defense." The winning team stops doing what put them in the lead and, instead, struggles to protect their lead, hoping to run out the clock before their opponent scores enough points to beat them. Sometimes it works. Often it backfires. It's a survival tactic.

Are we playing prevent defense? That's survival.

Thriving begins with developing a clear vision, implementing it, and then sticking with it. Without vision to guide us, we're vulnerable to the two standard motivators: getting pleasure and avoiding pain.

These ensure that we stay in the survival zone. We're inviting you to embrace another motivation—the power of a compelling vision.

When we truly know what we want, we can thrive.

## WONDER

So, how do we find out what we want? We start by wondering *what if?*

In their book, *The 15 Commitments of Conscious Leadership*, the authors state, "Effective leaders learn to get into a state of wonder on a consistent basis. What is wonder? To find out—and to see it in action—we need look no further than at a child.

"Before the age of six, children are natural wonderers. It's as though they move through the world saying, 'Hmmm, I wonder what this is or I wonder how this works—or tastes or feels or smells—or I wonder what happens if I do this?'

"Wonder is open-ended curiosity. It is asking a question for which we don't know the answer, and we don't know—or care—if there is one. Wonder is as much about the question as it is about the answer."[1]

We all know adults who haven't lost their sense of wonder about the world. They are fun to be around! It's a trait that successful entrepreneurs share and it's a key to moving from survive to thrive and staying there.

Wonder shifts life from duty to adventure. Even the best vision won't motivate for long if it isn't wonder-full.

## THINK BOLD

Vision must take shape in relationship to the way things currently are. This requires a particular kind of intelligence. F. Scott Fitzgerald wrote, "The test of a first-rate intelligence is the ability to hold two opposed ideas in the mind at the same time, and still retain the ability to function."

One "idea" is the vision of what we want. The other is our current reality, the reference that we build our vision in relationship to.

If we start with the way things are it's too easy to get bogged down in troublesome details. In fact, that's a significant problem in many organizations—too much focus on the details of the day and no time for vision.

The pressure to survive can be an excuse not to thrive.

When we start with a vision of what we want, we stand a better chance of returning to the very real challenges of here and now without getting overwhelmed. Crafting a vision and assessing reality—in this order—is a tactical necessity.

In his book, *The Path of Least Resistance: Learning to Become the Creative Force in Your Own Life*, Robert Fritz wrote, "If you limit your choice to only what seems possible or reasonable, you disconnect yourself from what you truly want, and all that is left is a compromise . . . The human spirit will not invest itself in a compromise."[2]

Developing a compelling vision, in relationship to something specific in your life or organization, requires using your imagination. You have to think bold.

## IDENTIFY THE VISION

Identify what you want to create a vision for. As an example, you may want your shipping department to be more efficient. Or, you might want your son to get better grades.

Let's work on the organizational challenge first. We'll return to the personal example shortly.

Begin to wonder. What would it mean for the shipping department to function more efficiently? The tendency will be to answer that question with details. "Deliveries are made on time. Customers are happy. The dispatchers are less stressed."

All well and good and these results may prove a vision has been realized, but they are not the vision itself.

The vision is a declaration.

For instance: "Our shipping department is the most efficient in the business."

That's lean. You can fill in the details later.

The vision is tightly focused, powerful, and definitive. There's no doubt about what you want.

Be as specific as you can and think in the present tense, first person. And, think bold. As the saying goes, "Shoot for the moon. If you miss, you'll land among the stars."

Better yet, note this comment from Oliver Wendell Holmes: "A mind that is stretched by a new experience can never go back to its old dimensions." Using your imagination this way will stretch your mind, for good.

A compelling vision always involves a stretch. If it's too easy, it won't be compelling. If it's too much of a stretch it can break.

Your vision has to be believable to you. You won't suddenly be able to fly. You won't increase sales by 600% overnight. You won't lose thirty pounds in a week.

The ideal vision can be described as a "believable stretch." For instance, you might envision increasing sales by 15% over the quarter, you could lose ten pounds this month, and you certainly can book a flight!

**SAY IT, SEE IT, FEEL IT**

There are three components to crafting a vision capable of holding your interest and enrolling others as stakeholders.

First, you need to say it, as we just did, in a few potent words. Most of us have participated in brainstorming sessions, pouring hours into discussion and flip chart work, finally coming up with a vision statement that someone read, someone typed up, someone sent to the team, and everyone filed.

A vision statement—however brilliant and inspirational—will not motivate on its own, at least not for very long. But it's a start and it's absolutely necessary.

Back to our example: "Our shipping department is the most efficient in the business." Notice again how simple this is, just one sentence—worded in the present tense—conveying one goal already achieved.

It's a done deal, not something you are aiming for in the future.

This kind of intention setting is hardly a new idea. So, are you doing it? We've found there's often a disconnect between knowing about this principle and actually employing it.

If you can't readily remember what your personal or corporate vision statement is, you're not using it.

## SEE IT

"Seasoned athletes use vivid, highly detailed internal images and run-throughs of the entire performance, engaging all their senses in their mental rehearsal, and they combine their knowledge of the sports venue with mental rehearsal. World champion golfer Jack Nicklaus has said: "I never hit a shot, not even in practice, without having a very sharp, in-focus picture of it in my head."[3]

Even duffers visualize their shots. We know it helps. And we know it works best when we get as specific as possible. Why? Because the more accurate our intention is the more likely our mind/body/heart will be convinced it's real and serve us faithfully by delivering up the result we want.

We're setting up a conflict, deliberately, between the way things are and the way we want them to be. The challenge is to make that vision real . . . to ourselves.

"Natan Sharansky, a computer specialist who spent nine years in prison in the USSR after being accused of spying for the U.S. has a lot of experience with mental practices. While in solitary confinement, he played himself in mental chess, saying, "I might as well use the opportunity to become the world champion!" Remarkably, in 1996, Sharansky beat world champion chess player Garry Kasparov!"[4]

Back to our example.

"Our shipping department is the most efficient in the business." That's what you're saying.

What you're seeing might be something like this:

"It's February 15, next year. I'm sitting in my office at 6:00 p.m. with Cathy and Jim. They just told me that we met all our goals for improving shipping. Cathy reads a letter from a very happy customer whom we solved a delivery problem for. Jim uncorks the champagne and we toast our success."

Notice how specific this is:

- You have a date.

- You have a firm result.

- You have details about the scene—the letter, the champagne.

- You can add in sounds, smells, thoughts, anything to help make your vision as real as a memory.

**FEEL IT**

The third step is to feel it. Here's the way *not* to do this: "I will feel great!" That statement won't create anything for two reasons—it's worded as a future possibility and the word "great" is too general.

You want to describe what you are feeling as an experienced reality with more specific words. "I feel great!" is a start but "I feel thrilled," or "I'm really, really stoked that it turned out to be such an enjoyable team effort," are much better.

**ABOUT YOUR SON**

Let's not forget about your son. And this brings up an interesting question: Is it fair to create a vision for another person?

It's fine to create a supportive intention. For instance, in this case it could be something like: "I'm supporting Marco to be happy and successful at school."

It's up to Marco to list the specific results *he* wants, but you're committed to creating an environment that enhances the odds that he'll more fully embrace his own potential.

Now, what do you see? "Amanda and I are sitting with Marco in the den. He's telling us that he's doing better in school and thanks me for helping with his homework."

How does that feel? "I'm thrilled, so proud of Marco, and it's great that we've gotten so much closer by working together this way."

## HOW TO SAVE A COMPANY

A friend, Ben, told us this story about how he averted a potential disaster in his company. His top sales generator, Jim, showed up one day during a critical period in the organization's growth and announced that he was quitting. Ben knew that losing Jim could cripple the company.

Much to Jim's surprise, Ben didn't get angry or beg him to say. Instead, he asked about what was happening in Jim's life.

Ben learned that Jim had financial troubles. As Ben explored deeper, he learned that this poor guy was working six days a week, driving many miles every day in an old gas guzzling truck in hopes of generating more sales commission. His wife was angry and felt deserted in the marriage; she was threatening to leave him.

Ben had an insight and made a simple connection. "Why doesn't the company pay to convert your truck to natural gas?" he proposed.

The conversion to natural gas saved Jim hundreds of dollars a month, allowing him to stay home on Saturdays. His wife was thrilled and their marriage revived. Jim withdrew his resignation and worked with Ben for many more years.

Ben had a vision for his company that didn't include losing his highest performing sales person. His compelling vision of success was so strong that two things happened:

1. He came up with an innovative insight that led to this imaginative strategy.

2. His confidence infused Jim with a renewed commitment to the company.

## PROOF OF VISION

Proof of vision is found in the results. A properly developed vision will *always* get results.

Those results may not be exactly what you had in mind because there are a million factors beyond your control that will influence the outcome. In fact, the physical result may turn out to be radically different than what you hoped for.

But you *can* achieve the feeling you expect that success to give you. This introduces a vital distinction with our process. We champion achieving the *emotional* result you want to enjoy from the result, not just the physical result.

You use your stated vision as a target to aim for, but proof of vision comes from experiencing the feeling.

Does this let us off the hook from doing the hard  work necessary to reach our goals? Not at all. But it filters our choices. Committing  to feel *now* the way we hope to feel when we succeed gives us a compass.

That compass will guide us and help us live our values, rather than sacrifice them to achieve a possible future result. When we experience our desired result now, that feeling allows us to gauge whether or not we are truly in alignment with what matters most.

It's possible to achieve a physical result—for instance, you might succeed in making your shipping department more efficient—but you also alienate your team by micromanaging and control tripping. So, you hit your numbers but does it feel successful when your team shuns you?

In our story, Ben had a vision pulling him forward, Jim didn't. Jim was surviving; Ben was thriving. But Jim was open for change and when he met with Ben they thought collaboratively to come up with an answer to the problem.

It took both of them, one being inspiring and the other being inspired.

Vision is no substitute for work. But it makes work more enjoyable, more effective, and easier. And a compelling vision, experienced emotionally long before physical results show up, keeps you motivated.

## VISION = CONFIDENCE

In his book, *Powerhouse CAA—The Untold Story of Hollywood's Creative Artists Agency,* James Andrew Miller tells of how Michael Ovitz and his partners broke away from the William Morris Agency in 1975 to form their own agency.5

Industry professionals were convinced they'd lost their minds. Who would leave William Morris to compete with such a behemoth?

Ovitz's vision was absolutely clear. He would request ten minutes of time from the studio heads, actors, and other talent he wanted to bring into CAA's fold.

Before their meeting began, Ovitz would take off his watch and set it on the table in front of him. Because of his clarity and passion—delivered in just ten minutes!—Ovitz began bringing new clients on board.

So convinced were Ovitz and his partners that they could provide an unprecedented level of service and care for these clients that they didn't even require them to sign a contract.

They told their new clients that if they failed to provide them with an acceptable level of service they wouldn't try to keep them on board. They only wanted clients who truly *wanted* to be their clients.

It worked.

Ovitz grew his new agency, CAA, into the world's leading talent agency, representing actors like Tom Cruise, Dustin Hoffman, and Barbara Streisand. CAA also represented directors like Steven Spielberg, Barry Levinson, and Sydney Pollack. Not bad, considering they started with a $21,000 bank loan and their wives working as receptionists!

How would you craft and sustain a vision like Ovitz did, one that others would eagerly embrace? And how could you maintain it and spread it through your organization and family?

Say it, see it, feel it.

## YOU CAN'T GET THERE FROM HERE

I (Will) was shopping with my wife the other day. We couldn't find a particular item in the store and finally asked a clerk. "You'll find that on the second floor," she instructed.

We could have continued wandering around the first floor until closing time and never found what we were looking for. We had to change levels. When we did, there it was.

Thriving will remain an impossible dream as long as we are committed to surviving. Until we put vision first, until we rise to that level and stay there, we won't find the success and happiness we are looking for.

Put vision first—the way we've explained it—and watch what happens in your life and in your organization.

## CHAPTER FOUR INSIGHTS

| SURVIVING | THRIVING |
|---|---|
| Not knowing what you want. | Being crystal clear about what you want. |
| Playing "prevent defense" to try and limp towards a win. | Continuing to do what made you successful and forging towards fulfillment. |
| Hanging on to certainty that blinds you to novel solutions. | Using wonder to alert you to innovative possibilities. |
| Clinging to one right thing and being defensive to ward off threats. | Holding two opposing ideas at the same time and remaining functional. |
| Assuming you know your vision but never speak of it. | Clearly writing and speaking out your intention and goals. |
| Being overwhelmed by details of everyday tasks. | Seeing into a future where you have succeeded. |
| Feeling the "slings and arrows of outrageous fortune." | Feeling the reward of your success ahead of time. |

# Chapter Five:

# Results Now

*My mission in life is not merely to survive,*
*but to thrive; and to do so with some passion,*
*some compassion, some humor, and some style.*

~ Maya Angelou

Pam was a 36-year-old social worker who sought help from me (Will) to figure out what to do with her life. She felt like she was at a crossroads, both personally and professionally. Plus, she had some serious health problems.

As always with new clients, I began by introducing vision. I coached her in the basics. It turned out that she was a natural. And, she was disciplined. She practiced every day.

She decided to work on an event coming up in a few weeks, a panel she was presenting on. She created her vision of what it would be like —her ideal result—and she got very detailed about what it would look like. She also dialed into the feeling she hoped to have with a successful event.

We scheduled a call for the day after the event. It turned out to be quite a session.

She reported three significant occurrences. First, the event went off great. Couldn't have been better. Second, she told me that it felt exactly how she had imagined it would.

Thirdly, and this was a big surprise, she had several people approach her afterwards to say that she was almost glowing! And that's how she felt.

We mused on what might explain this phenomenon.

Out of the blue, I uttered a word I seldom use: "Fusion!" Her *anticipated* feeling joined with the *real* feeling and BOOM, energy was created.

Other clients have reported similar stories. I have no explanation for this but reports suggest that something tangible happens when vision meets execution.

## RESULTS MATTER

If we don't actually achieve results it calls our methodology and our abilities into question and rightfully so. But success is never just about *our* efforts. We're always dependent on others and we can't control them (although we may try).

How then can we increase our chances of achieving success when it's never just up to us? There are two strategies that help. First, make success a visible, present time experience that inspires others. Second, take action.

## I'LL HAVE WHAT SHE'S HAVING

If you remember the restaurant scene from the film *When Harry Met Sally*, you'll recall that when actress Meg Ryan faked an orgasm at a diner, a woman sitting in a nearby booth told the waitress, "I'll have what she's having."

She didn't ask, "What's she having?" She didn't care. What mattered was the result. She wanted what Ryan's character was having because of what it did for her.

Likewise, you want the result you are visioning because of how it will make you feel (plus many other benefits, but emotion is the motivating one).

We all know people who exude success. I (Will) always enjoy seeing John, a fitness trainer at the gym where I work out. Every time I ask John how he's doing he replies with a variation on the same theme: "Fantastic!"

And he clearly means it! He's having that experience, even if he's still tired from a 20-mile bike ride.

John motivates his clients with enthusiasm. They all want what he's having! It's an easy thought process: "Hmmm, John is always saying he's feeling fantastic and he seems to mean it. He works out a lot. So, maybe if I committed myself to working out regularly I could feel fantastic too."

**SHOW IT**

It's not dishonest to prematurely advertise the results you're going for. But you have to back it up with follow-through. John works out!

We've all known positive thinkers living on top of the world until reality brought them down to earth with a crash. Just feeling successful won't create success, regardless of what those self-help books tell you.

Talk with successful people. They will always tell you that they put in their hours; they did the work.

The point of living the feeling prior to achieving the physical result is to motivate you to take the necessary actions that will get those results. In the end, it's primarily the work you do that will produce the results you get, but the vision motivates and guides you.

And, showing how you feel will inspire others.

**TAKE ACTION**

Some people dream their lives away and never achieve anything. Others keep their nose to the grindstone and have no time for vision. The journey from survive to thrive requires a healthy balance: dream and act . . . together.

The most effective way to marry the two is to visit your vision regularly and take simple actions that will contribute to achieving the results you want.

Keep it simple while you're learning this process. Building a website is not an appropriate action choice for starters. It's too complex. When you first experiment with linking vision to action, pick one small and easy task, something you can check off by the end of the day.

Set yourself up for success. Make one phone call, send one email, or invest 15 minutes on a relevant task

Later, you can set up larger visions for strategic plans, building that website, etc. But for starters, committing to one simple task a day is a powerful new habit.

*Visit your vision . . . assign an action.*

Over time this will become an automatic reflex.

Along the way, you'll discover just how much time you have wasted in the past, thinking about doing something but not doing it. Instead, use this process to run through your vision and connect an action step, then do it that day.

So much for procrastination.

Again, the key is to keep this simple. Set yourself up for easy success that you can build on. Don't decide to do 40 push-ups every morning. Do five *this* morning.

**START MIDSTREAM**

It's tough to break inertia. It's easier to keep going once you've started. So, instead of sweating about starting in on some seemingly burdensome duty, start midstream.

If you have a list of ten things to do in order to achieve the results you want, take inventory of what you've already done. Expand your list from ten to fifteen and check off the first five. Suddenly you're a third of the way to your goal! It's a simple trick that really works.

I (Will) used to enjoy weeding in a large vegetable garden managed by my friend Peter. The garden provided produce for 150 people in the educational community where he lived.

I was a frequent visitor and remember how he always advised new helpers to face backwards towards what they had done, not forward towards what they still needed to do.

This let us enjoy the results we'd already achieved and motivated us to go for more. This also reframed our experience of "results.

There was no need to wait.

## REFRAMING RESULTS

The old paradigm for results is captured in the phrase "The end justifies the means." On this basis, everything is fair game; everything can be sacrificed to achieve a future outcome.

That's a survival model . . . and not everyone survives.

It can be a disaster in business, where an achieved goal burns out your team. It can be a disaster in personal life. Some of us can remember so-called "vacations" where jamming in as many attractions as possible turned leisure into work and fun was sacrificed to fill up the photo album.

The new success paradigm can be stated as "the means determine the end."

Whatever we do along the way will show up in our results. We can learn to enjoy the process, to treat everyone well, and refuse to wait for an emotional reward tied to some distant aim. We can celebrate our results now. We're no longer just working to achieve a future goal. We're also enjoying the process that's taking us there.

## A PRACTICE RUN

Let's walk through the steps of combining vision with results to shift from survive to thrive.

1) Identify the results you want.

2) Identify the results you want.

3) Create the vision (say it, see it, feel it).

4) Connect vision to results by committing to an easy action.

We'll provide an example to help you create your own. Use pen and paper to sketch out your strategy.

## 1. IDENTIFY THE RESULTS YOU WANT

We'll start with a career example. Let's say you've been toiling in a particular job for a while and you're overdue for a promotion. You're ready to advance but no one seems to notice. So, the result you want is clear—you want a promotion.

That is the *primary result* you want but there are also *secondary results*. If you were to focus only on the primary result, you might just walk into the boss's office and demand a raise. That could work. It might not.

Here's a better strategy.

Come up with more results than you want. For instance, you want to be appreciated. You want your work to be acknowledged. You want to be seen as a valued employee, and you want to come across as a highly prized contributor.

Continue thinking along these lines. Write a list of the results you want. Expand from one to many. What's in your results bundle? What do you *really* want?

## 2. CREATE THE VISION

Now that you've got an expanded understanding of what you want, you can go ahead and create a compelling vision that will help you generate those results. Remember our visioning formula: say it, see it, feel it.

### SAY IT

The vision statement is important. In this case, it could be something like "I'm celebrating my promotion and being appreciated as a highly valued employee." Notice, your vision statement is in the present tense and first person. You're stating it as a done deal.

Write it down. Take a few minutes to edit and concentrate meaning into a minimum number of words. Too much verbiage dulls the impact.

You want to be able to memorize your statement so you can repeat it to yourself whenever you have a moment, like when you're stuck in commuter traffic or waiting on a download.

**SEE IT**

Where are you for this celebration?

Picture your future success in such rich detail that it seems real. "I'm sitting in the family room with my husband. I've just given him the good news and he h with joy. Both kids come running into the room. We get out the ice cream and snuggle on the coach."

You can add more detail every time you run the vision. It's all about making something imaginary seem real.

**FEEL IT**

How will it feel to get that promotion? How will it feel to be appreciated, to be seen and valued? There are hundreds of emotion words but we tend to get stuck on just a few. Grow your emotional literacy.

Instead of imagining you will feel "great" or "relieved," get more creative. How about "thrilled, euphoric, grateful, nourished, sensational, tremendous, fabulous, delighted, free, jubilant, glorious?"

**3. CHOOSE AN ACTION**

As you complete running through your multi-dimensional vision, come up with one simple action you can take that will move you towards your goal. Commit to doing that and make sure you check it off before the day is done.

Remember to make it easy to succeed. *What* you do is less important than the momentum you're generating by *doing* it. At this early point your priority is to develop a new habit—connecting vision with action.

Now your vision can guide you because you've identified the results you want plus the rewards you want from them. By employing this process, you'll be using your brain's powerful reticular activating system to work for you as it sorts through your daily experience searching new opportunities that coincide with the vision you've created.

Keep this vision alive and experience the results. Every day.

## CHAPTER FIVE INSIGHTS

| SURVIVING | THRIVING |
|---|---|
| Waiting for results. | Results now. Allowing yourself to fully experience the emotional rewards along the way. |
| Pondering and wishing. | Taking simple actions each day. |
| Making success difficult to achieve, dependent on achieving only a certain kind of result. | Reframing success to focus on what you can influence and control, which includes how you feel. |
| Being obsessed with one result, making it your only gauge of success. | Identifying secondary goals and expanding your definition of success. |

# Chapter Six:

# Vision First—Results Now!

*Dreams don't work unless you take action.*
*The surest way to make your dreams*
*come true, is to live them.*

~ Roy T. Bennett

I (Will) am 21 and it's midnight at the sawmill.

My brother and I work the dry chain, stacking lumber as it shoots out in an endless stream. It's a grueling job and we're on the graveyard shift.

So, why are we having so much fun?

Our scruffy crew has turned work into play. We've become a team playing a game, determined to beat the record for board feet stacked in a shift. We fly around the chain, shouting instructions to each other, and watch in delight as the chain speeds up to bring us more lumber to pile.

We succeed!

We break production records, much to the surprise of our red neck foreman. Occasionally he strides from his hut to watch these crazy hippies working their tails off.

One night we get hungry. We order pizza and cokes. I remember the headlights of the delivery car stabbing through the blizzard, veering between giant piles of lumber, finally locating our shed and the driver getting out to deliver several giant pizzas and a case of soda.

We stop the chain. Nobody stops the chain. Ever. But we do.

The sudden silence is deafening in the snowfall. We sit on our stacks, munching and drinking. Foreman Bob storms out of his office, ready to fire everybody.

He takes in the bacchanalian scene and pauses mid-stride, mid-obscenity. We intuit his inner dialogue.

"Wait a minute. If I discipline them they're probably going to stop performing so well. My numbers will go down. I'll have to answer for that." He turns and retreats without a word.

It's a moment of victory we will never forget!

One of us takes him a slice later, after we restart the chain. We earned that break and our reward is much more than pizza, it's the intoxicating feeling of genuine empowerment.

We are Kings of the Universe.

## EMPOWERMENT

What motivated us to work like that?

I didn't know it at the time but we were enjoying the immediate benefits of what we now call, some forty years later, "vision first, results now."

What was our vision? To have fun. To change an awful job into a game.

What were the results we wanted? To break production records. But so what? We didn't expect to get a raise or an award. We were working our tails off for a different result.

Pride. Joy. Friendship.

There we were in the cold, wet, dark. Underpaid, overworked and . . . having a blast!

Imagine your team doing that. Imagine your teenage son doing that, with his homework and his chores. Imagine everyone empowering themselves!

We were enjoying the results we wanted then and there. We were proud of ourselves for breaking the record, we were joyful, and our friendships went ballistic.

These were teammates, not just other lowly laborers struggling to survive the shift while wishing we were somewhere, anywhere, else.

I'm sure foreman Bob thought we were nuts, but he didn't interfere, even when we broke the rules. At some level, even *he* knew that we'd earned our reward.

We didn't start off planning to shut down the chain for a pizza break. We just wanted to have fun. I'm sure boredom was the big motivator!

We had a vision, pretty simple. We experienced the results we wanted. Right away. And that is the secret to Vision First, Results Now.

Let's consider this principle as it applies to our challenges at work and home, using the biggest example we can think of.

## THE TITANIC PROBLEM

The woeful fate of the Titanic, a ship considered to be unsinkable, has long been referenced as a symbol for arrogant overconfidence and blindness to real risks.

The tragedy unfolded as the ship sped through iceberg-infested waters. By the time the lethal berg was sighted it was too late to turn and avoid hitting it. The collision sank the great ship.

There are important lessons woven through this story that can inform us about how to perceive and address our (much smaller) challenges.

## WHAT'S YOUR SPEED?

Some people rush through life, others dawdle. "Perfect speed" is a term coined by Richard Bach in his book *Jonathan Livingston Seagull.*

He wrote, "Heaven is not a place, and it is not a time. Heaven is being perfect. And that isn't flying a thousand miles an hour, or a million, or flying at the speed of light. Because any number is a limit, and perfection doesn't have limits. Perfect speed, my son, is being there."[1]

We all know that feeling of "being there," finding our groove where everything becomes effortless, timeless, and where perfection is not a linear measurement but an unmistakable feeling, one that we wish would last forever.

It never does, but we can learn how to nudge ourselves closer to it and how to sustain that zone when it happens, long enough to navigate around a problem, prevent it entirely, or leverage it into an asset.

I (Will) and my friends did exactly that at the sawmill. Time was dragging. The shift went on forever. But when we turned work into a game, time flew.

Einstein explained his Theory of Relativity this way: "Put your hand on a hot stove for a minute, and it seems like an hour. Sit with a pretty girl for an hour, and it seems like a minute. That's relativity."

## COURSE CORRECTION

The Titanic was going too fast. Work on the timber chain was going too slow.

We (Will) needed to speed up to hit "perfect speed." The Titanic needed to slow down to course correct in time to miss the iceberg. Why didn't they?

"Many Titanicologists have said that the ship's captain, Edward J. Smith, was aiming to better the crossing time of the Olympic, the Titanic's older sibling in the White Star fleet. For some, the fact that the Titanic was sailing full speed ahead despite concerns about icebergs was Smith's biggest misstep."[2]

The captain had a vision. He wanted to break a record.

My (Will's) team had a vision. We wanted to break a record too but that was a secondary reward for us. The primary result we wanted was to have fun. And we did.

That required being super-present, totally focused on what was happening moment by moment. The captain was focused too, on the result he wanted later. For him it was Vision First, Results Later.

That's what sunk the ship.

Imagine if he'd made breaking the speed record his secondary result and focused more on experiencing the feelings he wanted, and believed would come, from besting The Olympic in a way that delivered that result right away.

We can wonder, might he have taken the iceberg warnings more seriously and slowed down?

## MISSING THE OBVIOUS

The mass of the average iceberg lies 87% underwater. The same principle applies with problems. What you see is only, as they say, "the tip of the iceberg."

We've heard that phrase and probably acknowledged the principle, but it's easy to forget when all you see seems harmless. When the deadly iceberg was spotted, it was too late to turn in time to avoid hitting it.

"Binoculars that could have been used by lookouts on the night of the collision were locked up aboard the ship—and the key was held by David Blair, an officer who was bumped from the crew before the ship's departure from Southampton. Some historians have speculated that the fatal iceberg might have been spotted earlier if the binoculars were in use."[3]

Oops.

There is always more to see. Sometimes what we miss is obvious, at least we realize that in hindsight. Do we have our metaphorical binoculars locked away somewhere? Ones that would reveal the resources and voices we may be ignoring.

That happens when we are not fully present. We're not fully present when we project our results into the future. This contributes to a "brain blindness," a condition that we explored in an earlier chapter.

"The Titanic received multiple warnings about icefields in the North Atlantic over the wireless but Corfield (the researcher) notes that the last and most specific warning was not passed along by senior radio operator Jack Phillips to Captain Smith, apparently because it didn't carry the prefix "MSG" (Masters' Service Gram)."[4]

## COMMUNICATION

Oops again. So, communication is important. Tiny omissions can prove fatal, as it did in this case. Again, there was a conflict of visions. That radio operator didn't interpret the message as urgent so he didn't inform the captain and kept sending passenger messages to a receiver in Newfoundland.

He was doing his job. They would be out of range soon so this was a priority for him. He, the captain, the look out, they were all on different pages.

That's often the way in our organizations. Everyone may be doing their particular job well, but without the cohesion that a shared vision brings, and without the understanding that brings results from the future back to the present, "accidents" are bound to occur.

## EAGER INQUIRY

Your inquiry into the deeper nature of problems (what's under the surface), traveling "upstream" to locate causes, will surface hidden issues. Why is your son failing science? Why is your shipping department struggling?

Technology has improved. "Radar and satellite Internet both play a big part in helping keep ships safe while in transit, and that while not every shipping line invests in state-of-the art equipment, most have what it takes to identify large icebergs."[5]

Sonar and radar identify threats invisible to the human eye. An effective leader proactively develops her own sensing mechanisms and employs available technologies into an "early warning system."

It's one thing to have gut smarts, it's another to use them. Intuition, hunches, analyzing probabilities, these are skills to aggressively develop for problem prevention. But it all starts with curiosity that prompts eager inquiry.

It took a perfect storm of miscues, incompetence, dangerous ambition, and arrogance to sink the Titanic. The article we quoted from lists ten reasons for its demise, and there are more.

It all makes sense in hindsight but none of this was known at the time of the disaster. That's a chilling reminder of how easy it is to miss the obvious, which we do habitually when we are seduced by the desire for results we have projected into the future.

Vision first, results now. It's both a preventative strategy and a real-time motivator.

## RECOMMENDATIONS

- Slow down

- Be realistic about what's required for significant change

- Learn about the hidden 87%

- Activate your radar for early problem detection

- Communicate; get everyone on the same page.

## THE REAL PURPOSE OF A CRISIS

Crises happen. Prevention, maintenance, and quick action can minimize damage but none of us are spared the "slings and arrows of outrageous fortune," as the Bard warned.

The question is, how do we handle those emergencies? We can just put out the fire and move on or we can learn from what happened and develop protocols to improve operations.

Charles Dughigg, author of the *The Power of Habit,* reflects on how one of the most memorable calamities of the 1980s lead to a major turnaround in the U.S. space program.

"Good leaders seize crises to remake organizational habits. NASA administrators, for instance, tried for years to improve the agency's safety habits, but those efforts were unsuccessful until the space shuttle Challenger exploded in 1986. In the wake of that tragedy, the organization was able to overhaul how it enforced quality standards."[6]

An unexpected crisis might completely sabotage the fulfillment of your vision, if you let it.

Had NASA not held strongly to their vision in the wake of the disaster they could have easily given in to the many voices that called for them to scuttle the entire program. Instead, they regrouped and revamped. In a little more than two years, the shuttle Discovery was launched successfully, proving that even a devastating failure need not be the death knell for one's dreams.

Maybe the form of your vision will change but what about the feeling? You can remain flexible about your results. After all, you're not in control of everything, but you can be proactive about how you feel and make course corrections to stay on track.

In fact, that's your compass.

For instance, if the success you're working towards will give you the feeling of increased friendship with your team (one of the rewards I [Will] got at the sawmill), you will remain loyal to that feeling and refuse to sabotage it when, for instance, someone on the team screws up.

We've probably all been dressed down for making a mistake. Did that help? We're already feeling bad. We screwed up! What do we need from our supervisor? Not verbal abuse. That diminishes friendship.

Let's say you're the supervisor. What's your intention? Certainly, the mistake needs addressing. But how? You really want to accomplish three things:

1. Deepen friendship through difficult, honest communication.

2. Discover how to fix the problem and prevent another similar mistake.

3. Strengthen the shared vision on the team.

If you remain aware of these priorities, your communication will be very different. In fact, you'll use an unexpected challenge to *increase* the feeling you want. You'll actually get more of the result you want and right now.

That's magic. It's also money.

My (Will's) friends and I increased profits at that sawmill, and we didn't need to share them because we created our own reward. Imagine your team being motivated like that!

And imagine being able to handle serious crises in ways that turn out to be blessings in disguise.

I (Chris) learned this best from a former colleague of mine who seemed to flourish in the midst of chaos. When things would start to go sideways on a project, Rick would smile, his eyes would light up and then he'd look at the rest of us on his team.

"Now *this* is going to be fun!" he would say excitedly.

That simple reframe set a tone for the rest of us and provided me with a model I've applied many times since then. When our minds are lit up with an air of excitement and fun, we stand a far better chance of unearthing a brilliant solution during a challenging time than we ever would if we let the crisis determine our state of mind.

## A NEW VIEW OF SUCCESS

You're diagnosed with a deadly illness (just in your imagination!) and your doctor warns that you only have twelve months to live, at the most. After you get over the shock, you begin exploring resources, trying to find something, anything, that might extend your life.

While proceeding with whatever your doctor prescribes, you also learn that humor can be healthy, that laughing is good for the immune system.

So you begin watching funny movies, comedians on TV, you make a few new, light-hearted friends, and you distance yourself from the downers. You focus on the positive.

You have an amazing year.

Symptoms persist—even though you do everything you can to address them—but your whole quality of life changes. You're happy, even though you're still sick. Finally, you get to the appointed day . . . and you die.

What?

That's right. Neither the medical procedures you diligently pursued nor the weird idea of using humor as medicine made any difference. Wouldn't you be angry and disappointed that you spent that whole year being happy when you could have been miserable instead?

Really?

The crisis won. Was this failure? Yes, if living longer was your primary goal. No, if your primary goal was to improve the quality of your life, however long you had.

You were happy for the last year. That's a miracle.

Imagine the impact your choice to be happy would have had on everyone you knew, starting with your family. You would have been an inspiration, not just a burden.

We can't fix everything. Sometimes there's nothing we can do about changing a physical outcome. But we *can* change our experience along the way.

In the film, *Mr. Holland's Opus*, Mr. Holland is a music teacher who feels his life has been a failure because he never achieved fame as a composer. In the wonderful concluding scene, his successful graduates surprise him with a performance of his opus in the school auditorium.

Mr. Holland then learns about the wonderful careers many of them have now and realizes that his real success was that he inspired his students to succeed in life.

His assumed personal failure turned into a big, shared success.

## UNEXPECTED SUCCESS

We can't control everything. We *can* contribute our best, learn, and course correct as we go along.

When we take our cues from the feeling goal, not the physical one, we're committing to *living our values*, not being "successful" no matter what the cost.

This can create unexpected success.

Alfred Nobel, the Swedish chemist and engineer who founded the Noble Prize, unintentionally invented a new type of explosive after a laboratory explosion killed his younger brother.

The tragedy compelled him to seek a solution for the safe storage of volatile materials. But another accident, a can of nitroglycerin breaking open during transport, revealed an unexpected anomaly.

The packaging material for the cans contained a rock mixture called kieselguhr, which absorbed the nitro and stabilized it. In 1867 Nobel utilized his newfound knowledge to create and then patent his

invention: dynamite. [7]

We can only wonder what was going on for Nobel. Certainly, he was motivated by the tragedy of his brother's death. But he succeeded in an unexpected way.

We can adjust our speed to stay in our groove and be realistic about what's required for ongoing course corrections. We can proactively hunt for "the rest of the story" as radio personality Paul Harvey used to say, and we can communicate to make sure everyone is on the same page.

1.  Vision First—we create the result we want in detail and enroll stakeholders who will help us achieve our goals.

2.  Results Now—we determine what feeling our success will bring us and use this as a compass.

## CHAPTER SIX INSIGHTS

| SURVIVING | THRIVING |
|-----------|----------|
| Seeing life as hard work. | Seeing life as a game. |
| The Titanic problem—going too fast for safety. | Finding perfect speed. |
| Missing course corrections until it's too late. | Anticipating and adjusting course early. |
| Being unaware of the hidden aspects of a situation. | Inquiring and being proactive about learning what else is involved. |
| Failing to communicate. | Communicating accurately, fully, and in a timely fashion. |
| Being weakened by a crisis. | Using a crisis to improve performance. |

# PART THREE

## Expanded Awareness

*Where we assess the way things are,*
*harness the genius of inclusion,*
*and welcome the help we need.*

# Chapter Seven:

# Assessment

*I insist on a lot of time being spent,*
*almost every day, to just sit and think.*
*That is very uncommon in American business.*
*I read and think.*

*So I do more reading and thinking,*
*and make less impulse decisions*
*than most people in business.*

*I do it because I like this kind of life.*

~ Warren Buffett

Early on we told a story about three men driving to work who encountered a naked woman walking across the street in front of them.

Two of them misinterpreted what was happening. One of them figured out that she was sleep walking and helped her back to the safety of her home. He made the correct assessment.

## FACING FACTS . . . WHICH ONES?

All three men saw the same thing . . . or did they? Where did those different reactions come from?

They each made up their own unique version of the story, based on the meaning they imposed upon the facts. Same facts, three different stories.

"Situational awareness" is a term for describing the ability to notice what's *truly* happening free of your stories about what you see. High situational awareness can be developed by employing a kind of deliberate contemplation.

Warren Buffett spoke of this in the quote at the beginning of this chapter. This habit can improve assessment skills by reducing impulsive, reckless decisions, based on faulty interpretations.

## A THRIVING PRIMARY RELATIONSHIP

There is always a relationship between what's happening now and what you would like to have happen later. There is always a conflict present between these two so it's a challenging relationship by design. For most people, it's a survival relationship, but you can change that.

As far as the details of everyday living go . . . this is your primary relationship and it's meant to be a thriving one.

Discovering, articulating, and consciously growing a vision in business and life develops one side of that relationship; assessing the facts of your situation creates the other. You have to know your destination.

You also need to know your starting point.

Assessing and understanding the challenges you face, particularly the ones that appear to be significant obstacles to your success and happiness, is as important as crafting an experiential vision. They are equal partners in a thriving relationship.

Maintaining the status quo through unconscious busy work, ignoring the unpleasant realities and neglecting to tend your vision, is not a long-term success strategy.

Add to that the fact that things are changing faster every day and it's easy to understand how "overwhelm" interferes with developing this relationship. It's easier to just keep floating down the river, unaware and unconcerned for the moment that there's white water—or a waterfall—coming.

But, with vision in hand, you can be thorough in your assessment of everyday problems just around the corner, anticipate them, and be ready for sudden crises when they occur, as they inevitably will.

## FAILURE OR SUCCESS?

"Early in the 20th century, Kodak was an innovator in photography. By the time of the digital revolution, Kodak had gotten into a "we've always done it this way" trance. They had no incentive to listen to new ideas or promote innovators from within."[1]

In 1996 Kodak was rated the fourth most valuable brand in the U.S. Sixteen years later it filed for bankruptcy.

I (Chris) remember being invited into a series of meetings with the company as it became apparent that digital photography was on the verge of taking the world by storm. I convened a series of focus group sessions with various employee teams.

It quickly became clear that many of these loyal, dedicated, and deeply concerned individuals not only understood the tsunami of change that was nearly upon them, they were also full of viable and practical ideas for how Kodak could leap to the forefront of the quickly emerging digital revolution.

Sadly, in the follow-up meetings I attended, senior management didn't take their employees' suggestions seriously.

Too many of the top leaders were stuck on the old way—a way that had worked brilliantly for over 100 years. This was their established way of doing business and it had been their key to success . . . until it became the reason for their undoing.

Here's another example. Lynn L. Elsenhans became the CEO of Sunoco in 2008. "Demand for fuel was at a 27-year low . . . . To offset the losses, she cut personnel, sold or closed the firm's refineries and sold off unprofitable or losing businesses. During her term as CEO, the company value increased by 52%."[2]

The difference in what happened for these companies and the reasons why are obvious. One company assumed that a business as usual approach still applied even when a technological revolution was at their doorstep.

The other made tough, challenging decisions that enabled the company to survive and thrive even during challenging times.

So, let's get personal.

## DARING TO LOOK . . . WITH AN OPEN MIND

What's going on in your organization or family? Often, we're reluctant to look, to really look, and to face the truth, which we sense might force us into the unavoidable realization that change is needed.

It seems easier to avoid than confront, but there's a price tag on that (as Kodak, Swiss Air, Woolworth's, Sharper Image, etc., all discovered). Problems left untended become monsters that can overtake and sabotage operations or fracture family dynamics beyond repair.

I (Chris) grew up in a family that ran clothing stores and tailoring operations. I remember a saying that was often repeated there when someone had a seam that was just beginning to separate, "A stitch in time, saves nine." In other words, fix it as soon as you notice the problem or you'll be dealing with a much bigger issue later.

None of us like confrontation but it's always easier to handle problems when they're small, to face what happens *as* it happens. Just ask any repairman working on a water leak!

## A PROBLEM-SOLVING SKILLS MENU

To develop, sustain, and enjoy a successful life and career, we need to learn and master certain skills for managing challenges. This begins with crafting a vision, followed by making an honest and detailed assessment of the current situation.

Here are eight helpful protocols for your assessment process:

1. **Make a current assessment.** It's one thing to pay more attention to what's going on in a general way, it's another thing to regularly survey the situation in detail to track how you are moving towards the fulfillment of your vision . . . or not.

2. **Make a needs assessment.** What does the situation call for? Knowing as much as you can about the current situation, you can then begin to assemble your resources.

3. **Make an asset assessment.** What's readily available to address your problems? When you study what's immediately visible, you often discover surprises such as colleagues' skills you weren't previously aware of. The challenge literally calls those skills into visibility . . . if someone (like you) cares to notice.

4. **Map the field.** Remember to telescope back for a perspective view, so that whatever strategy you develop takes the big picture into account.

5. **Create and manage informal focus groups.** No one is infallible. Genius is meant to be cultured by the leader, not imposed. Soliciting feedback, rather than ramming through your own tactics, is a habit that engages stakeholders. It encourages everyone involved to anticipate problems and begin co-creating solutions, not waiting for the boss to issue instructions.

6. **Learn the art of the question.** Questions are a powerful method for surfacing issues and problem solving. Adopting the attitude that you would prefer to hear an answer from someone else rather than to voice one yourself, is a leadership style that grows more leaders.

7. **Learn the distinction between positions and interests**. This is a key to creative solution engineering, where you invite others to abandon individual positions in favor of shared interests that lead the way.

8. **Have the courage to call out where we're wrong**. If others are aware of a problem but unwilling or unable to speak up about it, your own willingness to do so will make a difference.

**START HERE**

Many consultants begin by focusing on how to fix problems. We don't take that approach. We start with an area that may need attention and then look to find what's working before tackling the challenge.

Similarly, we encourage our clients to develop the habit of regularly catching people doing things right. Then, if something isn't working, they'll have developed better rapport with their team and the foundation of trust needed to delve into it productively.

If your son brings home a report card with three B's, and A, and an F, talk about the A first. How did he get that A? Perhaps that same approach could be applied to improve the F.

If you need to talk to an employee about how they mishandled a situation, find something positive about them to begin with. If you're exploring a challenge, start with the vision of what you'd like to see. Next, dive into discussing all of the assets (including people's talents and abilities) that could make that possible. Then look the challenges clearly in the face.

This positive-first strategy lights our brains and neurology up. It establishes a hopeful frame, an environment where insights can grow.

When you adopt this communication style with family members or colleagues, you quickly establish a reputation as someone genuinely interested in increasing what's already working, rather than placing blame and demanding better performance.

Guess which style gets better results?

**THE ASSESSMENT**

When we interview potential new clients, we begin by determining their degree of readiness for constructive change. There are four possibilities:

1. Doing fine, don't need help, thank you very much.

2. In crisis, emergency action needed, please help.

3. Problems are showing up, motivated to take preemptive action.

4. Eager to develop new, even more productive practices and preventative strategies.

Our goal is to help every person and business progress to category four. If someone thinks everything is already fine and they don't need help—that's category one—there's really nothing we can do for them.

Nothing inhibits progress like apathetic self-satisfaction.

Creating positive change requires working the tension between an honest assessment of the way things are (current reality) and the way you want them to be (your vision).

There's a term for this, "structural tension," coined by author Robert Fritz in his book *The Path of Least Resistance*. We mentioned him in an earlier chapter. He describes structural tension as a healthy tension that makes constructive change possible.[3]

## RESOLVING TENSION

Imagine stretching a rubber band between your thumb and your forefinger. The thumb represents your vision; the finger is your current reality.

At some point that tension will resolve (you'll get tired!) and one of those digits will move. Either the thumb will move towards the finger or the finger will move towards the thumb.

When you develop this relationship between the way things are and the way you want them to be, and when you stay strong in your vision, your current reality will be drawn towards it.

Conversely, if you're so embroiled in the day-to-day challenges that your vision is just a vague wish, current reality will neutralize vision.

Things will stay the same.

Keep that image of the rubber band in mind as we deepen this exploration.

## TAKE A SNAPSHOT

You can undertake your own assessment by simply observing what's going on and taking a snapshot. It's important to do this without blame or judgment.

Are your employees happy or grumpy? Is your husband irritable? Are your kids running wild? Do you hate going to work because the stress is never-ending?

What's *really* going on?

Starting with the obvious, you can discern what's missing and (here's the key) learn what *you* need to provide. This means being personally accountable.

In their book, *The 15 Commitments of Conscious Leadership*, Jim Dethmer, Diana Chapman, and Kaley Warner Klemp use a single horizontal line to demonstrate how accountability works.

Above the line: "I commit to taking full responsibility for the circumstances of my life and for my physical, emotional, mental, and spiritual well-being. I commit to supporting others to take full responsibility for their lives."[4]

And, below the line: "I commit to blaming others and myself for what is wrong in the world. I commit to being a victim, villain, or hero and taking more or less than 100% responsibility."

This makes your choice unavoidably clear.

Either we step up and lead by example, taking full responsibility for the way things are (and for visioning how they *can* be) or we don't.

## BABIES IN THE WATER

A story shared at workshops for youth, sponsored by the Universalist Unitarian Foundation, highlights another essential ingredient for accurate assessments.

While this tale portrays a tragic scene unlikely to ever occur in your own life, notice if there are any parallels to challenging situations you've encountered . . . ones that could have been solved more quickly by employing the simple, yet profound step eventually  utilized by someone in this story.

Once upon a time, there was a small village on the edge of a river. Life in the village was busy.

There were people growing food and people teaching the children to make blankets and people making meals.

One day a villager took a break from harvesting food and noticed a baby floating down the river toward the village. She couldn't believe her eyes!

She heard crying in the distance and looked downstream to see that two babies had already floated by the village. She looked around at the other villagers working nearby. "Does anyone else see that baby?" she asked.

One villager heard the woman, but continued working. "Yes!" yelled a man who had been making soup.

"Oh, this is terrible!" A woman who had been building a campfire shouted, "Look, there are even more upstream!" Indeed, there were three more babies coming around the bend.

"How long have these babies been floating by?" asked another villager. No one knew for sure, but some people thought they might have seen something in the river earlier. They were busy at the time and did not have time to investigate.

They quickly organized themselves to rescue the babies. Watchtowers were built on both sides of the shore and swimmers were coordinated to maintain shifts of rescue teams that maintained 24-hour surveillance of the river.

Ziplines with baskets attached were stretched across the river to get even more babies to safety quickly.

The number of babies floating down the river only seemed to increase. The villagers built orphanages and they taught even more children to make blankets and they increased the amount of food they grew to keep the babies housed, warm and fed. Life in the village carried on.

Then one day at a meeting of the Village Council, a villager asked, *"But where are all these babies coming from?"*

"No one knows," said another villager. "But I say we organize a team to go upstream and find how who's throwing these babies in the river."

## LOOKING UPSTREAM

The villagers finally addressed the cause, instead of just the effects. Here's how *you* can "send a team upstream." You begin by inquiring into why your problems have appeared. You treat them as symptoms of deeper problems.

For instance, looking upstream to find the causes for why things are the way they are will surely help you learn why employees are grumpy; you didn't just hire the wrong ones. Or maybe you did. But why did you hire them?

A key component in the assessment process is to look upstream to discern underlying causes, rather than sticking with downstream Band-Aid solutions.

Impulse actions—the kind billionaire Warren Buffet avoids—may generate quick results but they can also create a sabotaging lifestyle, where you put out one fire after another.

You *can* take a pill to calm an acid stomach but what caused the problem? Why did you eat that pizza at midnight? And what other long-term habits are contributing to your health problems?

You can fire someone or hire someone else. That's appropriate at times. But you can also inquire into what really happened, so you don't repeat the pattern.

Why keep putting out fires when you could become expert at fire prevention?

Then you can devote saved time to creating radical success in a fire-free environment. Of course, there will always be fires. Some are manageable, some are not. But finding the cause makes a fundamental difference.

## DETECTIVE SKILLS

Jack is suddenly under-performing and turning work in late. Why? Instead of a lecture and threats, some careful questioning might surface his chronic dissatisfaction at work. Perhaps he isn't being appreciated. Maybe he would be better utilized in another role. He might have a problem at home. He may just need someone to talk to about it.

Your husband seems depressed and is uncommunicative. You didn't forget your anniversary or his birthday. What then? He's OK with you working a lot but he may not be OK with you bringing your work home every night. How would you discover that?

The successful manager/spouse/parent/CEO is also a great detective. She is curious. She *wants* to find out why things are the way they are, what the systemic causes are. She understands that the issues showing up are symptomatic of problems in the culture; they're not merely personal.

Parents know this. Children surface issues for the entire family. It's not just the kids. Their behavior can be both personal and symptomatic of something happening in the shared family environment for everyone to face.

## HOLD THE VISION, ADDRESS THE SITUATION

You can position yourself in the middle of the urgent problems and struggle to fix them. Or, you can position yourself inside a powerful vision and draw those problems towards resolution. Either way, there's creative tension.

How do you resolve it?

Remember that image of an elastic band stretched between your thumb (representing your vision) and forefinger (representing your situation). Eventually, either the problems will collapse and the vision will grow or the vision will collapse and the problems will grow.

Hold the vision. Address the situation. In that order.

Watch your working or home environment steadily change to reveal the qualities of your vision. It requires courage to stick to the vision and honesty to confront the problems. Someone has to be personally accountable.

That starts with you. But it spreads.

1. Define your vision and remain aware of it constantly.

2. Face what's real in your everyday circumstance *as* it happens.

3. Stay strong in your vision and draw problems towards it.

## CREATE YOUR PITCH

I (Chris) remember when my colleagues and I first started to work our way into the movie and television industry. Our vision was clear, but we were naive about what it would take to be accepted into a tightly held industry built on relationships of trust and demonstrated competence. Fortunately, we were wise enough to seek out mentors to guide us and to open doors for us.

One of the lessons we learned along the way was to honestly assess what the studios and networks were looking for and then pitch them the very thing they were hoping to find.

As we began to perfect the art of researching and pitching, we met other new producers who were also seeking to enter the field. We helped each other, tested our pitches on one another and developed a friendly competition focused on enhancing our skills.

I remember meeting two of these budding producers in the lobby bar of the Peninsula Hotel in Beverly Hills. Let me take you back in time to that moment.

The Peninsula is crawling with agents, producers, and actors, as is often the case. The place is totally nuts, but a fun place to meet and soak in the ambiance of success.

On this occasion, as I enter the room, I nearly crash into the actor, Richard Gere, who's navigating his way across the room with a drink in each hand. Whoa! I dodge right and disaster is averted. We exchange knowing looks and he gives me a hint of smile to say thanks for not creating a scene.

I spot my two friends at a nearby table . . . they are cracking up with laughter at my near mishap.

I sit down and before I can utter a word, they launch into a story, describing a pitch they'd just delivered at Twentieth Century Fox. It obviously went well, because they're pumped with excitement. "Wisely," they tell me, "we took a seasoned producer along as a partner."

"He's the one who told us to assess the situation," one friend begins. "You know to really scope it out first." He's laughing as he speaks. I'm not sure if he is still thinking about my Richard Gere moment or is just jazzed about the meeting they've come from.

"We had totally researched what they were looking for," my friend went on.

His partner chimed in. "We assessed our asses off!"

I find myself laughing and smiling with them. Their enthusiasm is contagious.

"In fact," one partner continues. "We did it so well that we got a development deal using just five words!"

"What!?" I laugh. "No way! What were the five words?"

"Excalibur meets the Old West," he nearly shouts, and we all burst into laughter. If only it could always be that easy!

The lesson here? Do your research! Assess the situation so that you can adapt the vision you create to coincide with the reality you'll be stepping into.

And then, if you're looking to enroll others, create an irresistible pitch . . . one that's truly desirable because it aligns your interests, needs, and wants with theirs.

Bottom line: People who tap into authentic power take responsibility and show the way. They lead with vision and they are scrupulous with their assessment of what's really going on.

When that relationship is truly thriving—the one between vision and assessment—your life and your organization will be thriving too.

## CHAPTER SEVEN INSIGHTS

| SURVIVING | THRIVING |
|---|---|
| Being blind to what's going on. | Developing and maintaining high situational awareness. |
| Struggling to survive by fighting off challenges to achieve a single, future goal. | Growing a healthy relationship between the way things are and how you want them to be. |
| Procrastinating and ignoring the problems that need solving right now. | Adapting ASAP; a stitch in time saves nine. |
| Trying your best with random solutions. | Developing an up-to-date menu of problem-solving skills. |
| Watching over staff's shoulders and confronting them with mistakes. | Catching your people doing it right. |
| Failing to develop and sustain a vision. | Remaining aware of your vision constantly. |

# Chapter Eight:

# The Genius of Inclusion

*An inclusive culture brings a wealth of ideas, innovation,
and drive to the organization—which allows you to be
well-positioned to anticipate important market changes,
be more responsive to customer needs, and
build a solid foundation for future needs.*

~ Kate DCamp
*University of Michigan
Ross School of Business*

The Monday morning meeting is heating up.

Several of the more vocal regulars on the executive team are hurling around ideas. But it is clear they aren't seeing eye-to-eye about why their single biggest customer has just decided to place all their orders on hold.

During a brief pause in the debate, a seldom-heard voice breaks the silence. "They're having cash flow issues," Linda says hesitantly, almost as if she is asking a question. After all, she is just an administrative assistant. Her job is to take notes, not have an opinion in the boardroom.

"That's ridiculous," Mike scoffs. He's one of the more strident execs. "How could you possibly know that?"

Linda avoids his glare by looking down at her note pad. The meeting proceeds for another few minutes before Roger, the Sr. VP of Sales, interrupts.

"Wait a minute. Linda, what were you trying to tell us?"

Linda gulps, wishing she'd never opened her mouth. But Roger continues. "You know something . . . about their cash flow problem?"

Taking a breath, Linda holds for just a beat and then answers, "Yes, my cousin works in their payables department and I heard him talking to his wife about it at a family dinner last night."

"Holy crap!" Mike blurts out. "They're into us for over a hundred thousand dollars! Why didn't you tell me this before?" Linda's eyes dart to Roger for help.

"Well, hell, Mike," Roger responds. "If that's how you treated me, I wouldn't tell you anything either."

We've just witnessed an exercise in increasing inclusion.

Roger saw the virus of bias at play and he called it out. It was preventing Mike and others from seeing Linda's value. And bias, as you can see, is one of the primary causes of exclusion. We are, however, typically blind to our own biases and their impact. That's why we need to be the "Norton Anti-Bias Software" for each other.

Can you imagine how Linda's sense of self and her belief in her own genius would have been damaged further had Roger not stepped in?

We also describe this as the art of facilitating genius. It's a skill that is rarely taught or modeled in most organizations or families.

So, what is inclusion and why is it so seldom a company-wide practice? To answer that question, let's travel back in history for a moment.

## A HAPPY ACCIDENT

When the Equal Opportunity Act was officially enacted in 1972 as a follow-up to the 1964 Civil Rights Act, the EEOC (Equal Opportunity Commission) was created to oversee the Act's implementation. Employers in the United States who had not already adopted a policy of hiring from a diverse pool of candidates suddenly found themselves under scrutiny relative to their hiring and promotion practices.

As you can imagine, there were a host of mixed feelings within companies about the government mandating hiring policies. Most companies made an effort to comply with the EEOC's guidelines. Some did it simply to continue benefiting from government contracts.

In the decades that followed, many organizations found that the increased variety in their talent pool brought with it a richer mix of cognitive diversity (ways of thinking) and contextual diversity (ways of seeing the world). As this phenomenon grew, academic institutions like the University of Michigan, MIT, BYU, and UCLA took notice and launched studies to analyze the impact diversity was having on organizations.

What they discovered was eye-opening.

Their studies revealed that increasing the level of human and cultural diversity within a team simultaneously created a richer diversity of thought, perspectives, and approaches.[1]

This represented an increase in talent-based assets, as they are sometimes called, and explained why diverse teams in the studies became significantly more effective in both solving challenging problems and predicting future outcomes than their more homogeneous counterparts. This was particularly true if the practice of inclusion was *consciously* infused into their methodologies.[2]

As Six Sigma and other continuous improvement movements like Lean Management found more widespread adaptation, an intriguing corollary came to light: inclusion appears to be a fundamental requirement for successfully implementing these and other process improvement strategies.

Inclusion, at its best, means providing everyone within an organization ample opportunities to develop and contribute to the company's success. When done well, leaders and teams involve a diverse variety of people to assess problems, explore improvement processes, and generate solutions.

In our own work, we have discovered that without a well-integrated mindset of inclusion, management often flounders, attempting to solve problems or create new opportunities from isolated points of view.

These exclusionary "ivory tower" practices often skew new policies, rendering solutions untenable and problematic for those tasked with implementing what often turns out to be largely misinformed decisions. All of us have witnessed and participated in this kind of ineffectiveness, in our teams at work and within our family dynamics.

Ivory-tower thinking also sabotages one of leadership's primary responsibilities—to facilitate the genius of their own people.

All too often "group think" produces stale strategies and suppresses innovation. "Diversity-thinking," on the other hand challenges us to consider new perspectives, points of view, and approaches that can lead to breakthrough ideas that develop and sustain a competitive advantage.

## A STORY OF INCLUSION

An important aspect of leadership is being adept at enrolling those closest to a problem in solving it. This can include inviting individuals who know next to nothing about the situation into the mix, because their fresh eyes and ears save them from the tyranny of the known. They aren't infected with "forest-itis" (that all-too- familiar condition of not being able to see the forest for the trees).

I (Chris) recall being asked by a well-known semiconductor company to visit one of their silicon wafer manufacturing plants. My assignment was to assist the leadership team deal with a recurring and very costly issue.

I knew nothing about the process of manufacturing silicon wafers. That gave me an advantage. I brought a fresh perspective and different questions.

We began to explore the situation together.

The plant leader had assembled his A-Team, which included the plant's senior engineer, two line supervisors, and three senior shift managers. They talked with genuine concern for fifteen minutes about their urgent problem, one that only occurred during the graveyard shift.

I learned that the plant's well-automated process had somehow gone awry during the previous three nights, leading to damaging temperature fluctuations during a critical heating process. This morning was the third time this problem-solving team had assembled and they were totally frustrated.

The night before, they had even brought in their employees from the day shift to run the line and determine if there were any possible human-linked errors involved.

As I listened, a question arose in my mind. "Who haven't you invited into this meeting?" I asked.

Several team members were quick to answer, their voices laced with irritation. "We've got everyone here who needs to be here. This is our A-Team," they responded.

"Excuse me," I replied, "but with all due respect, your A- Team hasn't solved this problem yet. You just suffered another six-figure loss last night."

The room grew quiet and I repeated my question in a different way. "Who else could you bring into this room to enrich the mix with some fresh thinking?"

The tension grew palpable.

One woman on the team pointed out that no one from maintenance had ever been brought into these conversations. Several people immediately sneered at the notion that a janitor could help solve a complex problem that was even stumping the A-Team.

"Let's get back to solving this," one of the team members said, insinuating that I'd just taken them on a wild goose chase. "Exactly!" someone else responded. "We don't have time to waste."

Fortunately, the plant manager was wiser. He picked up on what was happening.

To the surprise of almost everyone, he stopped the meeting and called for Don, the graveyard maintenance lead, to join the meeting. Fortunately, who Don was just punching out and getting ready to go home, was happy to join us.

As soon as he was asked about the situation, Don shared that he'd seen a fluctuation in the power supply each of the last three nights. He pinpointed when the manufacturing errors had occurred. They had *all* occurred just moments after the power fluctuations. Don had informed his supervisors who told him that the fluctuations were unrelated coincidences.

But they weren't.

What Don had noticed was important. It turned out that by following his discovery further, the team was able to isolate and fix the problem . . . that same day. Bingo! And a powerful lesson about inclusion was learned.

Think about it. In this case, it took:

- An outsider (me) asking a controversial question.

- A plant manager moving beyond his team's skepticism to invite an unlikely person into the mix.

- An employee (Don) identifying the problem.

- This same employee, normally excluded from this level of problem solving, undaunted in his commitment to share what he knew, providing the A-Team with a missing piece of critical information.

The team's repeated failures to solve the problem occurred because their organizational culture did not value inclusion. Until this episode occurred they hadn't realized that they weren't mining the full genius of their organization.

## AN INCLUSION INVENTORY

Following this experience, a number of managers and supervisors at the semiconductor plant began to implement a new practice. Their number one agenda item for every meeting became what they called their "Inclusion Inventory."

This is the question they would ask before they began: "Do we have enough diversity in this room to address the topics, challenges, and opportunities we're about to explore?"

If the answer was no, then they covered other incidentals while a better, richer mix of people were invited to join them, including some employees who knew nothing about the topic under discussion.

What took place at this semiconductor plant was a rare anomaly. These types of scenarios play out regularly in all kinds of organizations. The inclusionary practices the leaders developed afterward, however, are still rare. In fact, whenever we first address the issue of inclusion with many organizations we work with, the customary pushback reminds us of this incident.

"Inclusion takes too much time," is what we often hear. "If you stop to ask everybody what color the wall in the breakroom should be painted," one manager complained, "we'll never get anything done."

This manager's comment, by the way, uses a strategy known as setting up a "straw man." The watered-down example he chose to challenge the efficacy of our recommendation was so weak that, had we defended it, he could have easily discredited our suggestion.

And that was precisely his intention, as he later confessed.

## THE INCLUSION CONTINUUM

Once they hear the story of the semiconductor plant, however, many of those who've seen inclusion as an "just another exercise in political correctness," begin to understand its practical value. It then becomes easier for them to see how their own unconscious exclusion may be costing them time and money as well.

And it's seldom lost on anyone that had the plant manager or his A-Team included Don in their conversation from the onset, and taken his unique vantage point into account earlier, they could have saved hundreds of man-hours and literally hundreds of thousands of dollars in wasted materials.

Where or in what circumstances might *you* or *your* organization be vulnerable?

The following diagram illustrates how the process of inclusion can be utilized to more deeply tap the intelligence of everyone in your organization. As you study this tool, begin thinking about who gets overlooked in your organization? Whose unique perspective might improve a decision-making process? Whose voice is missing from creative discussions? Who is it that often disagrees with your point of view that needs to be heard to ensure you are paying attention to the other side of the story?

## The Inclusion Continuum

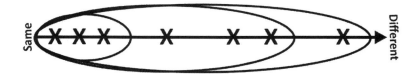

The left side of this continuum represents those with whom we are most comfortable (similar background, thinking or work style, similar level within the organization, similar discipline or skillsets, etc.). The right side represents those with fewer similarities, more differences, and even some individuals who may be difficult or uncomfortable to work with because their extreme differences seem challenging to manage.

Our tendency is to fill our teams of "go-to" people with those most like us in terms of how they think and how we prefer to do things. The practice of inclusion, however, means that we intentionally reach out to include a more representative sample of people all across the continuum.

This includes people who are closer to the issue or have unique perspectives. It turns out that they are often the ones who can help us understand implications we have missed and introduce novel ideas for resolving problems.

Notice that inclusion does not mean asking every single person along the continuum for their point of view on every single issue. Instead, we strategically look for those people with particularly good vantage points, especially those who may also have influence and rapport with their own constituent groups.

## THE "L" WORD

In addition to including a diverse range of individuals in meetings and inquiries for effective problem solving, there's another key ingredient required to effectively wrangle the latent genius of a group: the tone of our communications.

Think back to the story of Linda earlier in this chapter. She was present in the room, but more or less invisible. The dismissive way she was treated and the role she was cast in was such that it took a lot of courage for her to speak up. When she did, she was initially shut down.

How a person is spoken and listened to establishes an environment that encourages openness, creates safety, and invites engagement, or one that breeds cautiousness, non-disclosure, and compliant nods.

The wrong tone can instantly establish that what we're looking for is tacit agreement with accepted ideas within the status quo. That and no more.

No wonder Linda felt nervous to speak up!

It may be challenging to grasp for hard-charging leaders or managers, but genius is best cultivated in an environment of love and respect. We did indeed just use the "L" word. But we're not talking about romance!

We're talking about love in the broader sense as a shared experience of giving and receiving affirmation and appreciation. There is now an impressive volume of brain science to back up our assertion that love like this is a good business strategy.

Some readers might be tempted to set up a straw-man argument right now. It could go like this: "We don't have time for any touchy-feely nonsense. We can't let our people do whatever they damn well please and give them all trophies."

Or, the pushback could resemble a statement we often hear as we initially encourage leaders or managers to offer better and more meaningful praise and acknowledgment for their team's efforts. "I'm supposed to praise them for doing what we're paying them to do? That's ridiculous! Why should I have to do that?"

By the way, we heard those exact words from a corporate manager in a team meeting we facilitated on this very topic. Here's how we responded.

"Because it works!"

We went on to share with him that creating and maintaining an environment of love and respect is hard work. It takes an enhanced level of courage, clarity, and a genuine willingness to hold ourselves and others accountable.

Not everyone has the guts or developed ability to create such a culture. That's for sure. But the future—which arrived at your front door today, by the way—is requiring precisely this type of moxie from all leaders and managers who want engaged colleagues, not compliant employees.

Such an environment fosters transparency, trust, and openness, and encourages the generous voluntary sharing of a broad range of ideas and concerns. The result is always well worth the effort. That's not our opinion; it's the proof our clients report to us regularly.

## THE HIGH-PERFORMANCE EQUATION

Cultures of love and respect also breed loyalty and sustain high performance. By being positive, realistic, consistent, and fair, company leaders who master this approach make it easy for people to be at their best and to share their finest ideas openly.

I (Will) was interviewing successful entrepreneurs for a book I co-authored years ago and spent a couple of hours with a retired oilman from Texas. He was now living in Southern California and had become highly successful as a financial trader.

He told me about a crisis early in his business life. The night before a crucial meeting with a potential client, he learned that a big "No" was coming. He was furious. At that point, his leadership style was "Shoot first and ask questions later." He confessed that he was typically aggressive, angry, and often downright abusive in his negotiations. Bullying had worked for him so far and he had no intention of changing.

If anything, he thought he should turn up the heat and handle this coming rejection with even more macho force. Especially since this lost deal would jeopardize the very survival of their young business.

He was very motivated.

But something made him pause. Years before, he had made contact with a meditation teacher to help him relieve stress. He managed to connect with his teacher by phone, explained the situation, and heard this advice:

"Go to the meeting early, before anyone else arrives. As each person enters the room, greet them, connect eye to eye, and focus on these words silently: "I love you and I don't need anything from you."

You can imagine his initial reaction to this suggestion!

But he was desperate and he respected his meditation teacher so he decided to give it a try.

He described how difficult it was to face the first arrival this way but after the third person he was almost in tears. He felt something deep stirring in him, the actual experience of love, which had nothing to do with romance (a first for him)!

The meeting began and sure enough, they got their "No."

But instead of flying into a rage or resorting to heavy-handed manipulation, he found himself saying something like this: "I understand and respect your decision. But we do think we can help your company so here's what I suggest. If you would, please reconsider while my team and I leave the room for 15 minutes. And I'm dropping our fee from the 10% we'd discussed to zero.

"We don't want your money. We just want to help you. So, we'll leave, and you talk this over, and if you decide you'd like us to help you, we are willing to work with you for whatever fee you decide we are worth, from zero up to the 10%."

His colleagues almost went into cardiac arrest!

For one thing, they had never heard any sentiments like this coming from him before. And they freaked out about his offer. How could they work for free? Board members representing the potential client were likewise shocked, but they agreed to his radical proposal.

Only about ten minutes passed before they were invited back into the room. "We can't accept your offer," their spokesman said. "We've decided to pay you 15% on a trial basis, to see what results you can get. We are most impressed with your integrity and look forward to seeing what happens."

What happened was hugely successful.

They worked with that company for years, made millions of dollars together, and became family friends, attending each other's birthday parties.

This is an example of inclusion, in this case, a radical approach to problem solving that went against everything this gentleman had employed to be successful before.

Sometimes we need to include voices from those we have marginalized in our organizations, and sometimes there might be a personal voice we've ignored that has the genius wisdom we need for the particular challenge at hand.

The same principle applies in personal life. Consider your family dynamic. Who do you include when you discuss important decisions? Children are routinely excluded. They're kids, what could they contribute?

Why not find out?

Whether or not your six-year-old has anything wise to add is not the primary point. You're a family, bond through respectful inclusion.

## LOVE 2.0

In her book, *Love 2.0*, psychologist Dr. Barbara Frederickson explains our tendency in Western culture to define love as a private emotion. "Defining love, instead, as positivity resonance challenges this view," she states.

"Love unfolds and reverberates between and among people—*within* interpersonal transactions—and thereby belongs to all parties involved, and to the metaphorical connective tissue that binds them together, albeit temporarily. More than any other positive emotion, then, love belongs not to one person, but to pairs or groups of people. It resides within connections."[3]

As Frederickson and others have discovered through their research, love is actually a state of being that enhances our ability to be creative and responsive, to communicate and feel a sense of belonging and connection.

Like all states of being, we are literally able—through a process the Heart Math Institute calls entrainment—to transmit that state to others.

In other words, love is contagious.

As for the brain science, we just mentioned, you might recall from our comments in Chapter Two that the amygdala is the fight, flight, freeze, or faint region of the brain. It lights up when a person feels a sense of danger, foreboding, or banishment. As shown in the following chart, when an "amygdala hijack" occurs, energy and function that would normally be taking place in other parts of the brain, go partially offline.

### The "Amygdala Hijack"

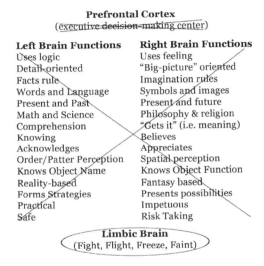

**Prefrontal Cortex**
(executive decision-making center)

| Left Brain Functions | Right Brain Functions |
| --- | --- |
| Uses logic | Uses feeling |
| Detail-oriented | "Big-picture" oriented |
| Facts rule | Imagination rules |
| Words and Language | Symbols and images |
| Present and Past | Present and future |
| Math and Science | Philosophy & religion |
| Comprehension | "Gets it" (i.e. meaning) |
| Knowing | Believes |
| Acknowledges | Appreciates |
| Order/Patter Perception | Spatial perception |
| Knows Object Name | Knows Object Function |
| Reality-based | Fantasy based |
| Forms Strategies | Presents possibilities |
| Practical | Impetuous |
| Safe | Risk Taking |

**Limbic Brain**
(Fight, Flight, Freeze, Faint)

The executive decision-making ability of the prefrontal cortex and multiplicity of our right- and left-brain skills and abilities are largely suspended when this hijack occurs. Work or home environments that create ongoing stress, a lack of feeling safe, or a sense of intimidation, exclusion, or banishment make it very difficult for our brains to remain fully online.

It's almost impossible under such conditions for most people to function at their best. But that's what happens when we create or support an environment that keeps people's survival center on high alert.

If we truly want to access the realm of genius in our teams, organizations, and families, the environment we sustain will make a huge difference. By the way, the easiest way to create and sustain an atmosphere of engagement is to catch people doing something right!

As attested to time after time through employee engagement surveys and leadership 360 feedback tools, this one simple act, done well, has a remarkably positive impact. In addition, offering immediate and specific praise when you see someone doing something well gives them a shot of dopamine that reinforces that behavior by strengthening that neural pathway.

We are always emanating some sort of "state"—a combination of our brainwaves (EEG) and our heart waves (EKG)—felt and adapted to via "mirror neurons" and through other modes of processing that quantum physicists are now exploring. The question is, are we personally willing to create and maintain a state that includes the right kind of communication, tone, and feeling that facilitates genius?

If so, we are beginning to master the art of inclusion—a practice that enables us and everyone we come in contact with to be more engaged, lit up, and contributing to the greater good of all concerned.

## CHAPTER EIGHT INSIGHTS

| SURVIVING | THRIVING |
|---|---|
| Approaching diversity as a potential liability, thus doing only what is absolutely required by law or policy to expand the differences to which you are exposed. | Seeing differences as assets and seeking to create more diverse teams and perspectives in order to optimize the level of cognitive and contextual diversity you have on-hand to solve problems and innovate. |
| Creating a group of regular "go-to" people who think like you to make it easier to come to conclusions while leaving out those who may see things differently. | Actively pursuing inclusion by seeking diverse viewpoints all along the way thus creating more well-thought out solutions that have better group buy-in. |
| Functioning as a compliance officer by assuming that people should do what they're being paid to do without any praise or additional recognition. | Catching people doing it right to reinforce teamwork, creativity, and collaboration and to help people build strong, new neural pathways for full engagement, satisfaction, and contribution. |

# PART FOUR:

## Power Up

*Where we reclaim our power,
assume quantum responsibility,
and focus our intention for success.*

# Chapter Nine:

# Dynamic Power

*Most people walk through the world
in a trance of disempowerment.*

~ Milton Erickson, M.D.

Melanie is adamant about her big idea.

The daylong celebration she's planning with the marketing team is crucial to how their organization will be perceived by clients. Even more important for Melanie, however, is her own hidden agenda. It's buried so well she can almost pretend it doesn't exist.

She desperately wants to be seen as someone primed to move up in the company . . . somebody with vision. And, she has a clear idea of how that can happen.

But Melanie's not paying attention. She's so tightly focused on her vision that she's not allowing her reticular activating system to fully assess the situation. Her team has big-time doubts about the musical artist she wants to headline their event in a closing concert, but Melanie doesn't notice them exchanging concerned glances. Nobody really wants to take her on.

Finally, one of them speaks up. "The day's already loaded with events," he says. "This concert idea, it's just too much." But Melanie is not taking "no" for an answer! Her ego has put her situational awareness on hold. Inclusion is not part of her current game plan.

Flash forward six weeks. The event goes extremely well, except for the closing concert. At the end of a long day everyone is tired and wants to go home.

The concert bombs. Only a handful of people attend, mostly out of a sense of obligation.

Melanie is furious. She feels betrayed. How could they? After the lengths she went to convincing this artist to detour from his tour for their event. She looks like a fool, she tells herself.

The next morning Melanie confronts her team. "You set me up!" she accuses them angrily.

## THE BLAME GAME

One of the most dysfunctional games we play in our families, corporations, political arenas, and pretty much anywhere you find people interacting with each other, is the blame game.

Most of us buy into the socially acceptable belief that celebrates victimhood. We have even found a way to convince ourselves that we are being compassionate, perhaps even noble, when we treat people as victims (instead of helping them reclaim their power).

Dr. Milton Erickson, widely considered to be the father of clinical hypnotherapy, referred to this troublesome malaise as the "trance of disempowerment." When we engage with others in that trance state, we deprive them of their dignity by creating patronizing models of supposed support. This denies all of us the deeper levels of healing and creativity available when we support each other as empowered individuals, not victims.

This reminds me (Chris) of an experience I had as an executive for an entertainment company. My colleagues and I became so fascinated with this debilitating phenomenon that we created a comedic game show pilot called "The Blame Game."

The idea was to run several rounds of questions and queries of contestants who could win by pointing the finger at anyone and everyone except the obviously responsible party. Our hope was that the hilarity of the game would begin to make it glaringly apparent how ridiculous and disempowering it is to cast people in the victim role, and how it escalates difficulties and unhappiness.

It so happened that one of the writers on our staff also wrote for Saturday Night Live. He innocently shared what he was working on with his fellow writers there.

They couldn't resist grabbing the idea.

The next thing we knew, a skit parodying our parody appeared on that wildly popular late-night sketch comedy show. It got lots of laughs . . . and it killed our plan to sell the actual show to anyone else, for a variety of legal reasons.

Our writer felt horrible. We felt worse.

Several days later, in a closed-door meeting with our other producers, we shared our initial reactions—frustration, then anger, and finally a sense of betrayal and victimhood.

How could he? How could they? Why, we ought to . . .

Suddenly, my primary partner on the project and I woke up to the irony of the situation. We began to laugh and we couldn't stop. We howled at how hilarious this was. Here we were, on the verge of becoming victims, right in the middle of making a game show designed to teach people how *not* to be victims!

Sure enough, our first instinct had been to point the finger at everyone but ourselves.

Not everyone immediately saw the humor in this. But you've got to love how life works. God is a jokester and is always teaching us how to have a sense of humor—while offering some pretty deep lessons about the power of responsibility.

## THE POWER SCALE

Back in the 70s, pioneering concepts about personal responsibility emerged from Werner Erhard and his est training. Many other explorers of the mind expanded upon his approach and morphed these ideas into very useful success models.

One of those innovators, Dr. William Guillory, showed me (Chris) a model that inspired me to develop what we've used in consulting Fortune 100 companies for nearly two decades.

To Dr. Guillory and others who pioneered this approach and have utilized it to change untold numbers of lives for the better we say, "Thank you!"

We call our model for dynamic responsibility The Power Scale.

It's very simple, based on the 0 to 10-point continuum shown below. It moves left to right from 0 for Victim (someone who's barely surviving) to 10 for Empowered (someone who's fully thriving). We list the qualities and behaviors associated with each side of the scale below.

## THE POWER SCALE

0                                               10

**Victim (Surviving)**             **Empowered (Thriving)**

| Victim (Surviving) | Empowered (Thriving) |
|---|---|
| Blame | Ownership |
| Excuses | Lessons Learned |
| Reactive | Proactive |
| Bias Cycles Prevail | Inclusive Views |
| Problem-Centric | Solution-Centric |
| Pessimistic | Healthy Optimism |
| Constricted Views | Expanded Awareness Catch |
| Point Out What's Wrong | People Doing It Right |
| Unhealthy Competition | Healthy Collaboration |
| Win/Lose | Win/Win/Win |

Under the Victim side of the scale are behaviors that we model when we've fallen into the trance of disempowerment. This describes the survival mindset.

Behaviors on the Empowered side are those typically demonstrated by people operating from a place of authentic vitality and power, those who thrive more  consistently.

Notice the last characteristic—Win/Win/Win—meaning we look for additional, non-obvious parties who might also benefit from whatever we are engaged in.

So, the question we can ask ourselves, especially in situations of conflict or drama is, "Where am I right now on the Power Scale? Am I thriving or surviving?

To do a quick assessment in any given situation, calculate your score by giving yourself one point for each behavior you exhibit from the right-hand side of the scale. Then subtract one point for each behavior from the left-hand side.

To be clear, we're not insinuating there aren't times to focus on the heart of a problem to discover reasons why something has become challenging. But you don't have to identify as a victim to do that.

What we *are* suggesting and strongly recommending is that behaviors on the left-hand side of this Power Scale tend to keep us stuck in survival mode. They preserve the status quo, even when (especially when) the status quo is no longer working. They keep us mired in the problem, whereas behaviors on the right side can free us to find a breakthrough.

## POWER UP!

It's easy to take responsibility for positive results when things are going smoothly and we're successful. However, whenever things go wrong, our tendency is to point the finger at others (or even ourselves), substituting blame and fault for responsibility.

That's the Blame Game.

Attempts to find fault and cast blame are actually strategies to escape responsibility and push ownership for problems away from ourselves and towards others. Self-blame is equally effective in avoiding responsibility.

The result? Nothing is learned and the cycle will almost certainly repeat itself. We know from experience that this is exactly what happens, over and over again.

This pattern can change.

The moment you or someone else begins to play the Blame Game, you've started slipping down the power scale towards zero. Take a look again at the behaviors on that end of the scale; they won't lead to anything productive.

Instead, it's time to power up.

This calls for a cold turkey commitment. Get out of The Blame Game, immediately!

Through coaching and consulting individuals and companies over many years, we've discovered four simple questions that help us exit The Blame Game. Using these questions for a self or team intervention can enable us to take our power back and infuse our interactions with vitality.

1. What is the outcome or solution I (or we) truly want or need?

2. What can I (or we) do to create that outcome?

3. Who and what resources do I (or we) need to involve or access?

4. What can I (or we) do about the elements that seem beyond our control (where or with whom do I [or we] have influence)?

By stopping and asking these four questions we shift how our brain is operating, from defensiveness and constriction to openness and expansion. We power up into a mindset of thriving, deliberately leaving our CYA (cover your ass) position and stepping into constructive collaboration.

"How can we right this ship together?"

While assessing how to address a challenge, we'll sometimes hear clients protest, "Well, I'm responsible for part of what happened, but I'm not the one who's really accountable here. That's Jim's area." Or, "We're in a matrixed system so no one has *all* the responsibility, it's distributed."

At this point, we tactfully refrain from shouting, "Are you *serious?* You're kidding me, right?" But it's no joke.

The remarkable truth is that most of us are truly confused about the most essential fundamental element of empowerment: our mindset.

## THE POWER OF OUR MINDSET

Dr. Guillory describes responsibility as a mindset or a state of mind.

If I see myself as the owner of the choices I make, responsible for the way I participate and for the results I generate on my own and in collaboration with others, then I will tap into and expand my capacity, abilities, influence, connections, and power to deliver an outcome.

By engaging this way, in a fully participative and responsible manner, I will also increase the odds of influencing others to power up. In addition, I'll dramatically improve our collaboration and improve our ability to generate the results we say we want or need.

On the other hand, if I see myself as only partially responsible for how I show up and for the results I produce, I'll exert only partial effort and only accept partial ownership (if any) for outcomes deemed less than satisfactory. That approach will keep me operating ineffectively, stuck in a victim loop and struggling to survive.

That's not thriving.

Similar patterns will continue to occur and I will continue to be a victim. Who would applaud a big-screen protagonist with that attitude and those behaviors? That has all the makings of a lousy story and a box office bomb!

If you want to immediately know where someone is on the Power Scale at any given moment, simply ask who is accountable when things aren't going well. The answer tells you which side of the scale they habitually occupy and which behaviors they are likely to exhibit when it really matters.

## FLIP SIDES OF THE SAME COIN

Heads or tails . . . we've all played that game of chance. Adopting a mindset of responsibility compels us to fully engage and take full ownership for the outcome. That tips the odds in our favor in a big way.

It's no game of chance anymore. In fact, being proactively responsible guarantees thriving.

Responsibility and accountability are flipsides of a winning coin. Responsibility is a mindset and accountability reveals it. A prevailing mindset based on the willingness to own results means being accountable for outcomes, whether successful or not.

You can hear the power of responsibility and accountability resound in the words of the Reverend Al Sharpton as he recounts his own background and the choices he faced.

"I could have easily been a statistic. Growing up in Brooklyn, N.Y., it was easy—a little too easy—to get into trouble. Surrounded by poor schools, lack of resources, high unemployment rates, poverty, gangs and more, I watched as many of my peers fell victim to a vicious cycle of diminished opportunities and imprisonment."

Rev. Sharpton chose a dramatically different path. We can see the genius in his words, evidence that he didn't identify as a victim. He *was* honest about what was happening but he made a different choice. Against tremendous odds, he succeeded in his life and has become an inspiration for millions.

He had his situation; we have ours. Life gets messy for all of us at times. What do we do about it?

When faced with a challenge or dilemma, simply ask yourself, "If I take responsibility for seeing this situation through to a successful conclusion:

- What do I need to do?

- Who do I need to involve?

- What are the elements that seem beyond my control?

- And, who will help hold me accountable?"

We suggest you use these four questions as often as you need to until the meaning of them integrates deep into your circuitry. Think of them like your quick reference guide for a software upgrade that takes a while to install. You're establishing a powerful new mindset of responsibility and accountability with each step.

## STANDING UPSTREAM

Maintaining a mindset of full personal responsibility encourages us to be proactive, to stand "upstream" where we benefit from a different perspective and see a bigger picture. This is the rock-solid stance we need to assume before making a decision, engaging in a project, launching an endeavor, or performing an intervention.

This perspective enables us to perceive the potential downstream effects of what we're about to do or say. As we engage with our colleagues based on this expanded awareness, we can explore additional options together by simply asking, "What could go right and what could go wrong?" When we do so, we allow our reticular activating system to focus on our vision *and* scan for potential opportunities and challenges before it's too late.

With a mindset of full responsibility, we also become more aware of the immediate impact our behavior will have on individuals and our organization. That's a powerful new habit to develop. Your ability to stand upstream and assess the potential downstream ripple effect is difficult, if not impossible, to develop without powering up to the high end of the Power Scale.

The kinds of questions asked, the presence and awareness generated, and the forethought that one naturally witnesses in people who occupy the upper end of the Power Scale simply aren't present in someone with a victim mindset.

Obviously so, because that victim end of the scale is a place of reactivity not proactivity.

You will certainly not be able to control everything and every person in your life or business. But by powering up and standing upstream, you'll significantly improve your ability to proactively respond to circumstances—including unexpected events and changes.

## ACCOUNTABILITY PARTNERS

If you're serious about powering up, keep a simple drawing of the Power Scale handy. Stick it on your wall or desk. Carry it in your purse or wallet. It's a great reminder.

When you find yourself in tense, risky situations, remember to consciously power up by asking those four questions so you can model the behaviors of a powerful leader, someone who thrives under pressure. This is how you cast yourself in a powerful new role in your own story, as someone being 100% responsible and accountable in every situation for every choice and decision.

Most importantly, find a friend to partner with you. You can help each other learn to live at the empowered end of the scale. It's as simple as asking each other, "Where are you on the Power Scale right now?"

When you have the time, you can go over the four questions together to help each other create a more powerful future, with new roles, new visions, and more fulfilling results. That's what happens when we support each other in upgrading the software of our minds and living out stories about thriving.

# CHAPTER NINE INSIGHTS

| SURVIVING | THRIVING |
|---|---|
| Playing the "blame game" by dishing out blame on yourself or others when things go wrong (i.e., avoiding responsibility), thus ensuring no new learning and the likelihood that you will repeat a similar scenario again. | Taking full ownership for the decisions you make and the outcomes you are a part of so you can benefit from both success and failure, thus learning from what didn't work and adopting best practices from what did work. |
| Being unwilling to stand upstream and consider the likely ripple effect or downstream consequences of your decisions and actions thus putting the short- and long- term outcomes at risk. | Consciously standing upstream and considering the likely downstream consequences of your decisions and actions in order to ensure the best short-term and long-term outcomes are realized. |
| Functioning solo or only with those who agree with you and are willing to allow you to continue "as is." | Having mutual accountability partners so we can hold each other to be the best we can be in each situation. |

# Chapter Ten:

# Resources

*Until we can receive with an open heart,*
*we're never really giving with an open heart.*
*When we attach judgment to receiving help,*
*we knowingly or unknowingly attach*
*judgment to giving help.*

~ Brené Brown

"Why do you cut off both ends of the ham before you cook it?" a child asked her mother during dinner preparations.

"I don't know," replied her mother. "My mother always did that. Let's ask her."

Grandma said, "Well, I don't know. My mother always did it. Let's ask her."

Great grandmother laughed and said, "The pan was too small."

When we ask for help, it's important to check whether what we receive has current value, or if it's just someone's antiquated habit that's become worthless today.

Something that made sense years ago may make no sense today. Habits your parents had are not automatically good for you.

**HELP!**

All of us need help to get from A to B. This chapter explores how to identify and leverage the resources you need. Help can come from unlikely directions. It can also seem to appear out of nowhere like something that isn't even on our radar screen. . . until it is!

What's the point we're making?

Life can pair us up with seemingly strange bedfellows (or collaborators) who may be able to provide precisely what we need, but not necessarily from whom or when we expect it. Help may also appear in a form that's different than we ever thought we needed.

Just such an unlikely matchup is sited in an issue of the Audubon Society's online news publication.

"Each year, 19 bird species inhabit the small 110-acre Shamrock Island Preserve in Corpus Christi Bay on Texas' southeastern coast. Because of soil erosion from winter storms, Shamrock Island is in poor condition and the Nature Conservancy is going to help—with the assistance of the largest oil and gas companies in the world.

"In what would first appear a strange match, Shell Oil has committed to providing $500,000 for the first phase of the $2.3 million restoration of the island."[1]

Author Michael Pollan gives us an even more inspiring example, this one from the natural world, chronicled in his 2013 article in The New Yorker called The Intelligent Plant.

"Citing the research of Suzanne Simard, a forest ecologist at the University of British Columbia, and her colleagues, (Stefano) Mancuso showed a slide depicting how trees in a forest organize themselves into far-flung networks, using the underground web of mycorrhizal fungi which connects their roots to exchange information and even goods. This 'wood-wide web,' as the title of one paper put it, allows scores of trees in a forest to convey warnings of insect attacks, and also to deliver carbon, nitrogen, and water to trees in need.

"When I reached Simard by phone, she described how she and her colleagues track the flow of nutrients and chemical signals through this invisible underground network. They injected fir trees with radioactive carbon isotopes, then followed the spread of the isotopes through the forest community using a variety of sensing methods, including a Geiger counter.

"Within a few days, stores of radioactive carbon had been routed from tree to tree. Every tree in a plot thirty meters' square was connected to the network; the oldest trees functioned as hubs, some with as many as forty-seven connections. The diagram of the forest network resembled an airline route map."[2]

That kind of synergistic connectivity is inspiring. It encourages us to ask questions like: "What kind of helping network am I developing?" or "How attuned am I to the often-subtle ways that Life opens an unexpected door for us?"

The days of The Lone Ranger are ending. Actually, even he had Tonto. And Silver.

True leaders are team players. They lead from within the circle and they make sure everyone gets credit for success. They understand the power of leveraging a group where everyone is an engaged stakeholder, helping each other in a playfully competitive way.

## LEVERAGING THE POWER OF A GROUP

We can do things on our own and make others go along with it—the old "command and control" leadership model—or we can build collaborative teams.

Guess which turns out to be more effective?

Too often we wait and only ask for help when we're frustrated, when we've tried everything and failed, or when we simply don't want to do something ourselves.

Delegating is supposed to be more than farming out what we don't want to do. It's about proactively leveraging the skills of those around us. In addition, we can leverage the power of a group.

Who's the group?

Could be your company, could be your family, could be a team you're playing on. Whatever the group, you can utilize the power of working together.

How many movies have we seen where a team saves the day—without billing for overtime! A crisis appears, people spring into action, petty squabbles are forgotten, and a larger purpose is served.

Smart leaders learn how to present requests for help or directions to staff as opportunities to face a challenge together, rather than the latest odious task they don't want to do themselves.

## ASK AND YOU *WILL* RECEIVE

There's a saying, "You can't win the lottery if you don't buy a ticket." Similarly, you're not likely to get help if you don't ask for it. So, what's your asking habit? Do you:

1. Ask in advance to make things easier?

2. Ask when you run into trouble?

3. Ask as a last resort?

4. Forget it, you'd rather fail than ask for help.

Let's reverse positions.

How do *you* feel when someone asks you for help? Remember a recent incident at work or in your personal life. Did you think whoever asked was stupid for not taking care of things on their own? Or did you feel honored that they thought you had knowhow or skills to help them?

You were probably glad to help.

## WHAT'S ON AND OFF YOUR RADAR?

Just as we tend to ignore, spurn, or fail to perceive readily available resources, we can neglect to reach beyond our own backyard, settling for limited options without realizing that we're setting those limits.

I (Chris) learned of this from a European client who was faced with a serious challenge regarding their expanding delivery routes.

Due to the introduction of several new industrial products, the volume and complexity of the delivery routes required to accomplish their distribution was taking twelve employees 24 hours to determine how to get the next day's deliveries lined up effectively.

Worse, the deliveries were often delayed or missed because of traffic snarls throughout the system.

In the midst of one of their intense scheduling sessions, a seemingly ludicrous idea popped into one of the scheduler's heads. "Ants!" he blurted out, much to his colleagues' surprise. "Where?" someone responded, imagining a massive invasion of six- legged creatures.

"No, no!" the scheduler laughed. He went on to explain that his friend was an entomologist, a Ph.D. who specialized in ants. He'd learned from him that ants create and run amazing distribution networks.

He posed an intriguing possibility: "Perhaps this ant expert could take a look at our system and see how it might be improved, using some of the methods that ants employ."

His colleagues howled with laughter. Surely this was another one of his famous jokes. But he persisted and they finally realized he was serious. And they listened, because nothing they'd tried so far had solved their growing dilemma.

There's a happy ending to this story.

By working with their friend's ant doctor, the delivery scheduling team developed a computer-run, GPS-based system, fed with live streaming data from drivers' vehicles. Suddenly they could observe traffic patterns and determine where and when traffic jams occurred. They also could study what alternative routes had been used successfully in the past.

They created a system that updated itself regularly, modeled on the ants who leave chemical signatures for their hive. Each driver's input fed into an overall delivery program. Like the hive mind of an ant bed, the system then automatically suggested schedules based on historical data that the schedulers could adapt as needed.

The system also enabled spontaneous re-routing to take place as new information arrived from delivery drivers out on the road.

The results were tremendous.

What had taken twelve people 24 hours to accomplish before was now accomplished by eight people in six hours. Better still, the delivery completion and on-time delivery rates increased dramatically.

As for the four employees no longer needed for scheduling, there were other jobs available for them in this quickly growing division.

The lesson here is that the answer to a problem threatening the viability of their business for months was, initially, totally off their radar.

Ants!

Who would've thought of ants? And who could have made that correlation, let alone voice it, had they not been part of a culture that encouraged and rewarded free-thinking? Help often comes from where we least expect it.

## A PRESIDENTIAL EXAMPLE

In 1961, in what is now a legendary moment, President Kennedy proclaimed that America would put a man on the moon and bring him home safely. He asked for help from the entire nation to pull that off and America responded.

It wasn't logical.

It wasn't some sort of well thought through strategy. It was a dream and it caught the imagination of our nation; the impossible was accomplished.

So, how trusting can *you* be when you ask for help?

If it's an emergency and you send out a distress signal you're not going to dismiss offers of help from *anyone* who responds. You won't decline assistance because you don't vote the same way or have a different religion.

The resources you need to succeed are available to you right now. Some may be unknown or unseen; many are obvious but underutilized.

With vision in one hand and your assessment in the other, you can reach out to welcome the help you need to reach your goals.

All of us need help to thrive. Asking for help is not a sign of weakness; it's smart and honest and the sign of a good team player.

## FAMILY

The same principles apply across the range of your personal and professional life but there are important differences. There is structure to your family life but it's less defined than at work where identifiable systems and processes guide decision-making. You typically can't apply that type of top-down, left-brained approach to your home life very effectively.

Millions of kids grew up in highly regimented homes and few of them report it was nurturing. Your personal life is the place for a more balanced environment. It's about family and love.

How many children report that their fathers were dictators? "My way or the highway" is the environment many kids grow up in. *Father Knows Best* wasn't just the name of a popular TV series; it's the shadow many of us grew up under.

A thriving home isn't autocratic, it's collaborative. Parents respect each other and invite their children to participate, not just follow orders. Family relationships are the perfect place to develop the practice of inclusion.

## A HAPPY EXCEPTION

I (Chris) grew up with a father who had a military background.

He always encouraged me to be a man of honor, something I'm still working on today. But what stood out to me most was his sense of equanimity.

Mom always had an equal voice in every discussion and decision. My brother and I were often consulted as well and we were also expected to handle our fair share of the household chores (dishes, ironing, cleaning, and so on).

When I complained to my father that my guy friends were asking me why I did "women's work," he looked at me earnestly and said, "If a man's masculinity is threatened by doing some dishes, he wasn't much of man to begin with."

I've never forgotten that moment and the tone he set throughout his life. He taught me by example that leading and living an honorable life meant treating people fairly and getting in the trenches with them when required (and doing it with gusto!).

If your home is not a thriving environment for your family, you can change that. In fact, you are responsible to develop a culture that grows happy, healthy children. Think about it; our future depends on them.

They are the leaders of tomorrow.

## SYMPTOMS

If you've ever had to deal with a water leak at home, you know the damage moisture causes over time. What starts as a tiny hole that allows rain to sneak under the metal flashing around a chimney or skylight can ruin an entire ceiling. And worse.

Caught early, it's an easy repair. Neglected, you're facing thousands of dollars in repairs and the inconvenience of moving out while the work is done.

It pays to detect symptoms early and take action. Likewise, with your life and organization, what signs are worth paying attention to?

How are you sleeping? How's your digestion? Are you gaining weight, losing weight, how are your stress levels? How is everyone else in your family faring?

What about morale in your organization? Any failed promises undermining confidence? Who needs appreciation?

Become a detective.

Look for clues as to what's (really) going on. Learn to tug on threads to see where they lead. Develop the habit of collaborative exploration. Make it a game. What's *really* happening?

Enroll your colleagues. Find out together.

When we're struggling to survive, we don't make time for this. We do if we're thriving. And it's what ensures we will continue to thrive.

## HELLO MOTHER, HELLO FATHER

Psychologist Carl Jung said, "Nothing has a stronger influence psychologically on their environment and especially on their children than the unlived life of the parent."[3]

This is worth remembering because every individual brings their parents along with them.

I (Will) remember Dad taking my younger brother and me car shopping with him when I was 14. I remember us watching Dad sitting in a 1964 Pontiac Parisienne convertible. The dreamy look in his eyes is indelibly imprinted in my memory.

He bought a Ford sedan but we know he kept dreaming about that convertible. His own father died when he was young. He went to work early to help support his family and never got to be that carefree guy rocketing down the highway with his hair blowing in the wind.

I carry that unlived part of his life in me. Every once in a while, when I cut loose, like hiking up a mountain and diving in an alpine lake, I remember my Dad and invite him to join me. Maybe in some other world he's getting a kick out of that.

The question is, what can we do with those unlived dreams we carry for our parents? For starters, we can recognize the tendency to live out similar patterns that our parents did.

It's more than genes. Habits flow through generations, often unquestioned.

We may keep cutting the ends off the ham, if you remember that story a few chapters back.

## SELF-INQUIRY

Why is this important? Because everyone has a BS meter to sniff out how authentic another person is. Someone who is weighed down by the burden of their parents' incompleteness isn't being fully themselves. It's like they're living in a haunted house and other people feel the ghosts.

A handful of helpful questions can help clean things up: How am I acting like my mother or father did? Am I treating my children the way my parents treated me? Can I change these habits?

Yes, you can.

It starts with recognizing what's going on, then making different choices. Success depends on sustained motivation, which takes us right back to the irreplaceable value of crafting a compelling vision to guide you.

## YOUR BEST FRIEND

Vision motivates, so does the support of a good friend.

A 2015 Australian study found that over half of the male respondents reported having no close friends. And, since the sixties, the male suicide rate has skyrocketed.

Three times as many men end their lives as do women. "The researchers found that male bonding is more likely to lower a man's stress levels than a night out with his partner, or time spent with the family."[4]

"Male bonding" is something we may joke about but it's vitally important to health and success at work. Sadly, we can live for years in a neighborhood or work for years in a cubicle without getting to know our neighbors very well.

Isolation is not only a problem for men. While women tend to be viewed as more relationship-oriented and share more openly with friends, studies show that women—in spite of the perception—often report a sense of deep loneliness as well.

Many women share that there's no one—including friends and family—with whom they can be truly open. Such loneliness increases stress and can contribute to serious health conditions. For today's women, heart attacks are now the number one cause of death.

Your best friend is not necessarily the one you feel the most comfortable with, like a drinking buddy, the girlfriends you go running with, or a childhood friend. Your best friend is the one who helps you grow your life in the direction you want.

If you're in a committed relationship, your spouse or life partner will hopefully be one of your best friends. We all need a champion to cheer us on, especially when we face challenges. What can you do to be a better champion of your loved one's life aims and vision?

If that's the kind of relationship you'd like to foster, there's no better place to start than with yourself. You are the first one deserving of your appreciation. And remember . . . what you appreciate, goes up in value.

As one of our friends stated recently, "Recognizing your own value is a truly selfless act. For in so doing, we understand more deeply the contribution we can make in the lives of others."

In another category, having a mentor, a coach—someone who can reflect back to you in ways that reveal the hidden implications in your decisions—is invaluable.

While there are skills to learn in being a successful counselor, the basic skill is listening, not giving advice. Some say that the listener controls the conversation. Listen, ask questions, and you'll be known as a great communicator. Plus, you'll likely hear something that can be of use to you.

## THE BUDDY SYSTEM

The buddy system has worked well forever. Having a friend, mentor, coach, partner, or spouse to support you is a powerful motivator.

Your buddy is more than someone to turn to in an emergency, they can function as a regular checkpoint for course corrections. And you can do the same for them.

Some marriages suffer, especially early on, when a couple first tries to navigate the notion of being exclusive. This process is often awkward or fraught with frustration as we learn that no one can be everything for another person.

Both of us are happily married and we have learned a healthy balance. We have strong friendships with many others.

Our wives appreciate that! They don't have to give us everything we need nor can we play every role for them. We have men friends and we have women friends. The same is true for them.

Because our boundaries are clear, our wives don't worry about our women friends nor do we worry about their guy friends. We love the power we see each other embody when we hang out with people who support us in thriving together.

People say it's lonely at the top. It's lonely on every level if a person isolates themselves from others. Relationships of all kinds take work . . . and play!

# CHAPTER TEN INSIGHTS

| SURVIVING | THRIVING |
|---|---|
| Ignoring the diverse range of available resources beyond your usual "experts." | Accessing all resources, especially the unlikely, to leverage the value of other, unusual perspectives. |
| Being exclusive and running a tight, hierarchical ship. | Being genuinely inclusive and treating family members and employees as valued stakeholders. |
| Maintaining "best friends" who support your established habits. | Maintaining best friends who help you grow. |
| Ignoring your inner life. | Acknowledging that you carry the unlived dreams of your parents. |
| Being a Lone Ranger. | Using the buddy system to get the support you need. |

# Chapter Eleven:

# Quantum Responsibility

*There are five fundamental qualities
that make every team great:
communication, trust, collective
responsibility, caring and pride.*

*Any one of these individually is important.
But all of them together are unbeatable.*

~ Mike Krzyzewski

Daniel strolls into the office lobby with a smile on his face. The social media campaign he set into motion early this morning was his best work yet.

There's just one little problem.

He didn't see a text message that came in just before the campaign clock started. The one that told him to abort!

And yeah, you're right . . . it's not a little problem. As a matter of fact, the finger pointing already started before Daniel even walked in the door.

"Why are you smiling?" Chelsea asks from behind the reception desk. Daniel stops in his tracks, puzzled.

"Oh jeez, you haven't heard yet," Chelsea says with panic in her voice. "Go talk to Ron."

The color drains out of Daniel's face. "Ron?"

Chelsea nods sympathetically.

As he heads down the hall to Ron's office, Daniel meets his friend Derrick. "Choose sides, buddy. It's hitting the fan, big time," Derrick warns.

"Sides?" Daniel asks. "What on earth is going on?"

## US vs. THEM?

We've been trained to take sides. It's a knee-jerk reaction. It means pointing the finger of blame at the "other side," at "them."

We've also been taught—even taunted or bullied—that choosing is urgent. Go! Now! Rush to one end or the other of a dilemma and stand firm in *our* position, championing *our* version of "the truth."

Then someone throws down the gauntlet. "You're either for us or against us!"

You've heard this polarized challenge issued more than a few times. Our egos are easily drawn into this trap. It's a deeply established habit that is especially virulent in crises.

But that's exactly where we need genius.

To access true genius, we can't allow ourselves to be painted into a corner with a declaration like "choose sides."

We're <u>not</u> inferring that "it's all good."

We're not saying that everyone should share the blame equally in all situations. In fact, we're not talking about blame at all.

What we propose and strongly encourage is intense scrutiny of the situation, curiosity and willingness to stand upstream and look downstream to understand cause and effect.

Together, we can survey the larger landscape and determine possible future consequences and ripple effects of our choices. Choosing sides means choosing to abandon personal and collective responsibility. When we don't take sides, we *do* take personal and collective responsibility for what happens.

Why does this work so well?

Remarkable things happen when we live our values and foster an environment that encourages a robustly intelligent search for innovative options.

It takes serious leadership chops to talk people out of playing The Blame Game. But the payoff is huge.

## EMPOWERMENT SQUARED

In a previous chapter, we invited you to take your power back.

We introduced you to a diagnostic tool called The Power Scale. As useful as this tool is for identifying whether your behaviors are empowering or disempowering you, it can be rendered ineffective by making one inaccurate assumption.

We'll explore this errant notion by diving more deeply into the story at the beginning of this chapter. As you read through this scenario, notice the assumptions your mind wants to make. Pay attention to which side you want to jump to and why.

## 3, 2, 1 LAUNCH!

Ron Dixon, the VP of Marketing for Pictogram, a new photo-posting site, doesn't tolerate mistakes. Especially mistakes that are client-facing. When he shows his marketing team his fresh idea for driving business to their newly revamped web app, he's on fire.

"I want this baby launched within the week," he tells them.

Tracie, the project manager for the website, expresses her concern. "I think we may want to wait a few weeks to make sure all of the kinks are worked out before we drive a lot of new business in," she says.

Several members of her development team give each other worried looks. They agree. She's right.

"Figure it out!" Ron replies. "I'm going to be presenting this campaign to the executive leadership team in the morning. I don't have time to do any hand-holding here. I need performance from you guys."

"What does that even mean?" Andrew, one of the programmers, whispers to his team. "We're not going to know how this app works under pressure till the traffic really starts hitting the site."

The meeting draws to a close amidst growing concern. But no one objects openly.

Daniel, on the other hand, is pumped. He loves Ron's idea and is stoked to have the chance to show the VP just how good he is at executing on big creative concepts.

Tracie grabs him by the arm as he's heading out of the meeting. "I'm worried," she tells Daniel. "If the site crashes during launch, it's going to get ugly."

"Well, let's touch base before it goes live," he reassures her. Tracie nods in agreement. Good idea.

The next morning, Tracie waits by Ron's office door. She's got to catch him before he goes to the executive meeting. As his door swings open he's on the move and she speeds along next to him, repeating her concerns.

"Dammit, Tracie!" Ron barks. "Just make it work. And if you absolutely must, then put the brakes on before it goes live. But you better have a solid reason why."

The evening before the launch, Tracie checks with Daniel and verifies that he'll be launching the campaign at 7 a.m. Eastern Time. That means if she's going to put the brakes on, she needs to do it now. "How late is too late?" she asks him.

"That's 5 a.m. our time," Daniel reminds her. "I'm going to stay up to ensure it all goes fine on my end. Ping me if there's a problem."

"OK," Tracie tells him. She then goes home, and continues to worry.

At 4:45 a.m. Tracie wakes up in a cold sweat. She's realized where the system vulnerability lies. She sends an emergency text to Daniel. "ABORT THE LAUNCH – IT'S NO GO!" Tracie breathes a sigh of relief and tumbles back into bed relieved that disaster has been averted.

But Daniel's fallen asleep at his desk at home.

At 5 a.m. MT the campaign launches as he sleeps. By 6 a.m. MT when Daniel awakens and checks in on it, the campaign's gone viral. By 8 a.m. MT the website is getting bombarded with new volume. At 8: 20 a.m., five minutes before Daniel strolls in the door smiling, the website crashes hard. Ron is livid! Heads are going to roll!

**WHOSE FAULT IS IT?**

Now that you know the story, we want to ask you a few simple "Agree" or "Disagree" questions. These are the type of questions Dr. Guillory uses in his work and they're designed to challenge our tendency to make decisions based on limiting beliefs.

1. Ron Dixon, the VP of Marketing is 100% responsible for the entire situation. Agree or Disagree?

2. Tracie is 100% responsible for not calling a halt to the project sooner. Agree or Disagree?

3. Andrew and the other web team members are responsible for the website crash. Agree or Disagree?

4. Daniel is 100% responsible for launching the social media campaign that crashed the site. Agree or Disagree?

With your answers in hand, we invite you to consider each of these statements again, this time, through the lens of a new context: What would best help the individuals in this scenario take their power back so that they make more intelligent, well-informed, highly productive decisions the next time around?

In other words, what if it's not about fault or blame, but about learning from what went wrong instead? What if it's about *each person* owning their role in the situation?

Imagine being asked to coach each individual involved. How would you advise them to respond to their statement in order to take their power back and engage their genius at the highest level possible?

Does this new approach change your answers?

For instance, imagine coaching Ron, the VP. Which answer for statement one—agree or disagree—would move *him* closer to 10 on the Power Scale?

Which answer would create a mindset that would lead him to tap more fully into his capacity to ensure that whatever he's set in motion turns out the way he wants it to?

Now, you might struggle with the notion that as the leader he is 100% responsible, because that would mean no one else is. "We don't want to let the rest of them off the hook." If you had that thought, you're not alone.

This is the number one mistake we've all been trained to make.

Remember that at the beginning of this section we warned that the Power Scale can be rendered ineffective through one inaccurate assumption? Here's the assumption, that there's only one single Power Scale shared by all those involved, and that responsibility must be divided up fairly in some way.

When we operate from that assumption we disempower everyone.

Everyone involved moves down the scale towards victimhood. Genius—our own and others—simply cannot survive, let alone thrive, in a culture of victimhood.

You've probably figured out the answer here: Everyone has their own unique Power Scale. So does each team, each department, and each organization.

This is the essence of Quantum Responsibility: we are each 100% responsible for our own role and for how we influence others in carrying out their roles.

As a refresher, take a look at the behaviors on each side of The Power Scale.

| Victim (Surviving) | Empowered (Thriving) |
| --- | --- |
| Blame | Ownership |
| Excuses | Lessons Learned |
| Reactive | Proactive |
| Bias Cycles Prevail | Inclusive Views |
| Problem-Centric | Solution-Centric |
| Pessimistic | Healthy Optimism |
| Constricted Views | Expanded Awareness |
| Point Out What's Wrong | Notice What's Working |
| Unhealthy Competition | Healthy Collaboration |
| Win/Lose | Win/Win/Win |

Stepping up to full ownership on your Power Scale takes nothing away from anyone else. In fact, it encourages them to step up and take their power back too!

Everyone involved can be at 10 on the Power Scale.

A VP's breadth of responsibility might be broader than a project manager because of their role and skills. But how the VP approaches their role, the influence they have, and the ripple effect their actions have on everyone in the entire organization can be similar.

Why?

People at 10 on the Power Scale act very different from those at 6 or even 8.

**LET THE POWER COACHING BEGIN!**

If Ron were to shift his mindset to 100% responsibility relative to how his decisions played out (all the way to 10 on the Power Scale), his odds for making successful decisions would be greatly enhanced.

How so?

For starters, Ron would have done a full assessment and utilized an inclusive process while developing his new campaign. He would have made sure that he understood what could go wrong and what the ramifications would be. Dissenting voices would have been listened to respectfully.

Ron would have also paid attention to Tracie's expressed concern the morning before the executive meeting. He could have still presented his plan, but with a later launch window. And he would have checked in along the way to see how things were going once the green light was given.

Does taking full ownership guarantee success? No!

But if their project fails and Ron's on the upper end of the Power Scale, he won't be as surprised. He'll be able set Plan B into motion in a timely manner and he'll also learn from what went wrong, rather than casting blame. That way, he and everyone involved can learn from what didn't work.

Failure to learn from our mistakes is one of the biggest reasons we suffer the consequences of Einstein's quote: "Doing the same thing over and over again, while expecting different results, is the definition of insanity."

Let's talk about Tracie.

Tracie is choosing to continue working with an unreasonable manager who doesn't listen to her concerns. She also made the decision to wait until the last minute to text (not phone) Daniel to call off the launch.

From having dealt with clients in similar situations numerous times, what we always encourage them to do is to get crystal clear about the likely future consequences of every choice and decision. Tracie knew that the odds were extremely high the launch would fail. But in spite of her reservations, she initially went ahead with it anyway.

This same dynamic played out when the Space Shuttle exploded in 2003 with five astronauts, a payload specialist, and a young teacher aboard.

Numerous people had expressed their concerns about the now infamous O-rings that failed and led to the explosion, but no one spoke up loudly enough to the right people until after the disaster had occurred.

What else might Tracie have done?

She could have gone to Andrew and the other programmers, then teamed with Daniel to predict possible volumes early on to convince Ron precisely why the early launch was too risky.

Also, we would have encouraged Andrew and his team to speak up in the meeting, not merely among themselves. Andrew could have approached Tracie and brainstormed with her as to how they could help Ron see the risk.

If they all saw themselves as the owners of the site's performance, what would they have done to ensure the crash didn't happen? How might they have influenced Daniel to stage the campaign differently?

Daniel—had he been willing to see himself as responsible for opening the flood gates that could crash the site—could have sat down with Tracie, Andrew and the team and figured out how to stagger their campaign so that it began small and grew as the site's dependability was incrementally verified.

Instead, he allowed his excitement for proving how well he could drive high volumes of traffic to the site to get in the way of considering the downstream effects of his efforts.

Disaster struck. But, as we are seeing, it could have easily been averted, if everyone had powered up and assumed 100% responsibility, rather than assuming others were "in charge."

## BACK TO *YOUR* LIFE

What does this have to do with your life and work?

Everything!

What if we all had each other's backs and rooted each other on at challenging moments? Or, what if we were all there to catch one another when we were on the edge of a poorly considered decision? Imagine the difference this approach could have on one of your projects . . . or on your family.

The key? No blame. 100% responsibility. For everyone. Each person has their own scale that applies to their own unique role.

## THE POWER THAT BINDS US TOGETHER

This is what Quantum Responsibility is all about.

Community, friendship, respect, and care for each other—the knowledge that our collective genius is at its best when we truly stand for one another—is a thing of beauty. And that kind of thriving is never a solo accomplishment.

In a thriving world, each one of us is individually and collectively responsible for the choices we make or don't make, whether those choices lead to success or not. It's up to us to step up, step in and learn from what went wrong, to leverage what went right even better in the future, and to seek the help we need to better understand the dynamics involved.

Constant improvement is the proof of personal and collective responsibility and accountability.

We are each responsible for the choice to take our power back.

And here's the tough truth: Life is holding us accountable whether we like it or not. There *are* ripple effects to *every* one of our choices, decisions, and actions. Eventually, though it may take some time, we reap what we sow.

So, if you decide it would be wise to hold yourself accountable the same way Life already *is* holding you accountable, then you might consider adopting a mindset of responsibility for:

- How you show up in relationship

- What your actions produce

- How well you set healthy boundaries

- How well you keep your word

- What you watch

- Who you listen to

- How willing you are to dig deeply for the truth

- How easily you allow yourself to be hypnotized, manipulated, propagandized, or unduly influenced by mainstream and social media

If you don't like what you discover in that personal assessment, beware of falling towards the disempowered side of the scale by shaming and blaming yourself.

Just own it and decide what you want to do about it, plus who you know (or can get to know) to partner up and help make the necessary positive changes.

Create a powerful vision and then invite others to live it with you.

We have an impact on many people every day. What if we paid closer attention to everyone we work with, live with, even to those we encounter in casual interactions?

What small but important actions could we take to make each person's day a little bit better?

Include them. Let them feel significant in your presence. Develop a reputation as someone who cares about others, a team player who welcomes all kinds of input and feedback.

## QUESTIONS FROM A ZEN MASTER

Our 21st century world appears to be coming apart at the seams in many alarming ways. It's tempting to bury our heads in the sand and act as if it will all get better on its own, but that just gets sand in our ears!

We prefer to adopt a simple, practical motto, one used by American Red Cross crisis workers to keep themselves grounded and focused in the chaos zone of a natural   disaster:

> *Do what you can*
> *with what you have*
> *from where you stand*
> *right now.*

Our families need us. Our friends need us. Our community, our workplace, and our nation need us. The world needs us. It's time for us—individually and collectively—to take our power back, one choice at a time.

Imagine what it could feel like to look downstream towards the possible future consequences of our responsible choices and know that we made the kinds of decisions that helped create a better  future, choices that our children and our children's children will be forever grateful we made. That's real commitment.

When asked how one can tell what they are committed to, a Zen Master told his student this:

"What did you do today? How about yesterday? What are you planning to do tomorrow? That's what you are committed to—that's what truly matters to you."

Taking full responsibility for your choices puts you in charge of the quality of your experience, regardless of what outside circumstances may present. And stepping up to 10 on The Power Scale also enhances your ability and odds of reshaping your outside circumstances over time to better conform to your vision and values.

## CHAPTER ELEVEN INSIGHTS

| SURVIVING | THRIVING |
|---|---|
| Creating false dichotomies that attempt to force people into choosing sides by employing either/or thinking and "us vs. them" posturing. | Encouraging both/and (a form of holistic thinking) as well as the notion that there is no "them." |
| Making or absorbing others' unquestioned assumptions and assigning motives to people to justify our point of view. | Questioning our assumptions and the inferences of others while looking more deeply into the motives and needs of those who disagree with us. |
| Dividing up the blame and distributing the accountability so that no one is truly empowered. No one is fully responsible but some people are more blameworthy. | Playing our unique roles in personally responsible ways. We are each responsible and accountable for our individual actions and choices and how they affect the whole. |
| Going on autopilot, acting as if mediocrity is acceptable as the status quo because so much is beyond our control. | Seeking to understand new ways to create excellent outcomes by doing what we can with what we have from where we stand right now. |

# Chapter Twelve:

# Empowerment Squared

*"I must do something,"*
*always solves more problems than,*
*"Something must be done."*

~ Major General Michael Jeffery

Steven stands at the podium delivering the last few words of his speech to the new division he's been charged with leading.

"You've heard my vision for this area of the company," he says proudly. "And now," Steven continues, standing up even straighter, "I empower each of you to do whatever it takes to get the job done— to bring this vision into reality!"

The halfhearted applause that follows his rousing call to action is not what Steven had expected.

"What is it with these people?" he grumbles to himself. "I thought they'd be excited to finally be given the authority to make things happen without a lot of management interference."

In the months that follow, it becomes clear that Steven's empowerment initiative is not going well. Some teams are running amuck with projects that are not in alignment with the company's intended direction.

On the other hand, managers in a number of departments complain that their people are hesitant to take even small steps without their specific approval.

Finally, in a one-on-one with Nadine, one of Steven's department heads, he's faced with a question he's not sure how to answer.

"What do you mean by empowerment?" Nadine asks, with obvious frustration in her voice. "It's a great word and all," she tells him, "but can you explain it to me . . . you know, how it actually works?"

## MORE THAN WORDS

Empowerment, in our experience, is one of the most misunderstood and misused words in the world of business, politics, or charitable endeavors. As a result, many people act as if it enabled them to wave a magic wand and suddenly empower people to perform feats that they were unable to accomplish just moments before.

"I empower you" or "You are empowered" are phrases that indicate a lack of understanding regarding what can be a very logical and straightforward process. Empowerment—when understood and properly applied—becomes yet another key ingredient of a thriving culture.

So, what is empowerment? And how is it applied?

## WHAT EMPOWERMENT IS AND IS NOT

Most people assume that if we delegate an assignment, we have *empowered* that person. Others believe that since they were supposedly *empowered* to carry out an assignment, they are now free to do it any way they please. Both assumptions can lead to trouble.

Empowerment is what occurs when an individual or group *chooses to* tap into their full capacity to solve a problem or achieve an outcome within the guidelines, authority, and parameters that they've been granted.

> ***Because empowerment is a personal decision,***
> ***it cannot be bestowed on another person.***

Empowerment can, however, be encouraged, supported, and stimulated by creating a culture of accountability where embracing empowerment is expected and required as a condition of employment or participation.

Generating empowered participation involves three components ("The 3 C's of Empowerment") that are essential for empowerment to fully function and be managed effectively. It is the job of the person who is granting authority or offering an assignment to ensure that these three components are in place:

1. *Capability* (cognitive, interpersonal, and technical skills)

2. *Clarity* (clear, written guidelines that are mutually agreed upon' what does success look like; how will we know if we're on track, etcetera?).

3. *Commitment* (as demonstrated by one's ownership of the outcome).

Let's explore each of these components more closely:

*Capability* means that a person has demonstrated that they are clearly capable of performing the assignment I'm about to delegate successfully, with minimal supervision or oversight.

If I am going to assign a project beyond their demonstrated capability, I need to ensure they have adequate training, coaching and/or mentoring to ensure they have a good chance to succeed at the "stretch project."

*Clarity* means that we have established clear expectations regarding an assignment or an ongoing task that is mutually understood and agreed upon. Wherever feasible, having such expectations in writing eliminates confusion and memory lapses.

Make sure that expectations include whatever support is available, their scope of authority and what the limits are, possible rewards, acknowledgment, consequences, etc.

*Commitment* means that each person involved is committed (in both word and deed) to engage their full capability in their respective roles to ensure that the outcome measures up to the agreed-upon guidelines for achieving the goal(s).

The essential ingredient for commitment is an experiential understanding of what it means to be personally responsible and personally accountable (i.e. assuming full quantum responsibility), as described in our previous chapters.

To be clear, while someone in a management, supervisory, or parental role assumes responsibility for ensuring these three conditions are present, the person accepting the new assignment or role has a corollary responsibility as well.

It is their job to ensure that their manager or supervisor has these conditions in place and to decide if they will or won't accept the assignment or opportunity that is being presented.

## CAPABILITY PRE-ASSESSMENT

As we described previously, a critically important part of realizing a vision is assessing the landscape between you and your goal or vision.

The same is true with any vision or assignment we have for our employees or team members.

In the workshop, based on their book, *Empowerment for High Performing Organizations*, authors Guillory and Galindo suggest that there are three areas to explore in determining a person or group's level of capability.[1]

### *Cognitive skills*

While this skillset category is often overlooked, a person's level of cognitive ability tremendously impacts their capacity to implement the other two skill-sets. When we are assessing this area, we pose these questions.

- What is the person's attitude?

- What's the story they've been generating?

- What limiting perceptions, biases, or assumptions do they tend to manifest?

- Do they understand the potential ripple effects of their action or inaction?

- Can they stand upstream and project likely future consequences?

## Interpersonal skills

This set of skills also comprises an area that we may have difficulty quantifying without the proper assessment tool, but we tend to know it when we see it.

- How well do they resolve conflicts?

- Do they turn professional matters into personal issues?

- Do they respectfully deal with differing viewpoints while still collaborating effectively?

## Technical skills

These types of skills have been euphemistically referred to as "hard skills." They are typically the most clearly understood and easily assessed elements of a person's capability. It is also the aspect that is most easily trained. Nevertheless, it should not be underestimated when assessing capability.

- Does the person have the training that enables them to apply a hard skill to *this specific* circumstance?

- What additional technical skills might they need to acquire to successfully complete this task or assignment?

- Who might they need to involve in the project who possesses a complementary set of skills necessary to fully reach a goal?

As mentioned previously, if you're the person taking on a new assignment or role, you should be asking *yourself* these questions to determine whether or not you're well-suited for the opportunity being offered.

**CLARITY PRE-ASSESSMENT**

Far too often, we assume we're being perfectly clear in terms of our instructions and expectations when, in fact, we're actually confusing those we're talking with.

Creating clarity in the following three areas enables us to ensure  that what *we've* said and meant and what *they've* heard are the same, that we've moved from vague to crystal   clear.

*Clear Expectation*

- Have I used clear, concise language that specifically defines the desired outcome?

- Have I asked them to repeat back to me their understanding of the assignment?

- Can they tell me what they will or will not do to achieve the outcome?

*Scope of Authority*

- Have I been clear on how much authority they have (be specific—"do whatever it takes" is not clear).

- Have I made it clear as to where and from whom they can get support or have questions answered should they so need?

*Accountability*

- Have I communicated any possible consequences connected with the assignment or requirement (the effect on others, rewards, acknowledgement, dis-incentives, etc.)?

- Can *they* tell me what the consequences are and/or the impact *their* performance will have on others and on themselves?

## COMMITMENT PRE-ASSESSMENT

This last area of pre-assessment is the one that some people find the most difficult to carry out, yet it is equally, if not more, important.

Why?

Because if someone has the capability and cognitive skills required but lacks the commitment to apply those abilities, any expectation we may have of their successfully carrying out their assignment is built on a faulty foundation.

*Roles*

- Have I been clear in terms of how my role intersects with theirs to support the accomplishment of the goal or assignment?

- Have I made it clear as to how their unique role applies to this assignment or requirement?

*Modeling Responsibility*

- Have I modeled taking full responsibility and accountability for my role and the support I'll provide?

- Have I walked through possible "what if" scenarios to assess their level of commitment? What will they do if this or that occurs?

*Stated Agreement*

- Do I have a statement of commitment from the person? For example, "Yes, I understand and I'm totally up for it. I'll keep you posted as we go."

Once again, we stress the importance of the reciprocal responsibility you have if you're the person being offered a role or new opportunity. You should be asking yourself if these conditions are present before you say, yes.

If they're not present, work with the person offering you the opportunity to get them in place. If they are resistant or unwilling to do so, at least you'll know what you're walking into and the level of risk you're incurring.

## IMPLEMENTING EMPOWERMENT

Once an assignment has been given, based on the guidelines we've just reviewed, the empowerment process is still only at the beginning phase.

Depending on where a person is along a continuum of cognitive ability, capacity to perform, and commitment, we need to manage the empowerment process differently. Dr. Ken Blanchard, in his book *Leadership and the One-Minute Manager*, refers to this approach as "Situational Leadership"[2]

Someone who is highly competent and fully committed, for example, requires very little oversight. They may simply need to keep you posted at certain milestones along the way or ask for your assistance should a problem beyond their scope of authority arise.

Another person who is very committed with great cognitive skills but who is not as competent in terms of their hard skills, may need more training or supervision by you or someone else in their area who can serve as a coach or mentor for them.

Though we probably wish it were not so, there are two other categories in the empowerment process that need a different approach when it comes to implementing empowerment.

One applies to the person who is highly skilled but not truly committed or who may have attitude issues. This person doesn't need close supervision in terms of their skillset but they may benefit from peer coaching or positive reinforcement as you praise them for using their skills well *and* having a good attitude.

The last implementing empowerment category relates to a person who lacks both skills and commitment. They need to be on a clear track to either turn things around (starting with their attitude and level of commitment) or they need to be moved into a different position that better suits their skills. They may even need to leave and find other employment, should their attitude issues or lack of skills not improve.

Knowing where a person is in terms of these four categories is accomplished through proper pre-assessments and follow-up.

Since empowerment is a challenging process that requires us to regularly operate outside our comfort zone, pairing people up with a peer coach/accountability partner is strongly recommended.

Examples of questions a peer coach might ask (or that you may ask yourself) are:

1. Are you generating the level of support you need to successfully accomplish the goal you've taken on?

2. Regarding your current assignment or task, how well have you assessed your own Capability, Clarity, and Commitment?

3. Do you understand the unique and simultaneous nature of your personal responsibility and group responsibility as it applies to your role in each situation?

4. What is required--beyond your defined job role--to improve chances for success?

5. Have you identified your previous limiting assumptions, biases, and preconceptions that could lead you to limiting behaviors and limited outcomes in this situation?

6. What can you do, who else do you need to involve, and what can you do about the elements that are beyond your control to ensure that this situation is properly resolved or this goal is met?

7. Are you willing to fully engage a peer coach? Have you created an accountability plan for yourself?

8. How well do you receive feedback and coaching? Are you defensive? Do you take challenging action steps that will move you out of your comfort zone and toward desired outcomes?

9. Are you acknowledging and rewarding your own incremental progress? Do you leverage mistakes as learning moments and apply the lessons learned for improved future outcomes?

By involving people inclusively in the process of developing the plans we have for them, we can also pre-assess their abilities in the various categories we've outlined. Empowerment works when we implement the empowerment process individually, based on which of the four categories people fall into and provide peer coaching or additional support as needed.

In so doing, we create an environment that enables individual genius to thrive.

If we could re-write Steven's story from the beginning of this chapter, pretending that he had instituted such practices, it might go something like this:

Steven stands at the podium delivering the last few words of his speech to the new division he's been charged with leading.

"It's been wonderful to go over the vision we've created together for this area of the company," he tells them. "Your input has been invaluable in making it potent and practical."

"Now I'm inviting each of you to engage your personal and collective genius in bringing this vision to reality. You have the capability and we've outlined each of your roles clearly. But if you have any questions as you move forward, talk to your manager or to me. I am committed to work with each one of you to ensure our success as a team."

In this version of the story we imagine genuine applause. This very different response to Steven's previous rousing call to action would have brought a smile to his face.

And it's easy to imagine a much better result, more aligned with what he was envisioning.

## EMPOWERMENT PRINCIPLES TO REMEMBER

1. While empowerment is a personal decision and cannot be granted to others, it can be encouraged, stimulated, supported, and modeled within a culture of accountability.

2. For empowerment to effectively take root, three key elements must be properly assessed and implemented: Capability, Clarity, and Commitment.

3. For empowerment to function effectively, responsibility must be seen as unique and simultaneous (i.e., each person is fully responsible for their unique role in any given situation).

4. While job roles are useful for defining our primary functions within an organization or team, they can also create unnecessary limitations when high performance becomes the standard.

5. Having limiting assumptions and preconceptions leads to limiting behavior or inactions and thus limited outcomes.

6. Being 100% responsible means, "What can I do, who else do I need to involve, and what can I do about the elements that are beyond my control to ensure that this situation is properly resolved or this goal is met?"

7. In an empowered setting, responsibility and accountability are flip sides of the same coin. "Responsibility is the mindset I enter a situation with, and accountability is my willingness to own the outcome—successful or not— without excuses. Such an approach generates tremendous learning opportunities and greatly increases the likelihood that one's full capability will be accessed to find a solution or to meet a goal.

8. Peer coaching and accountability partners are a highly effective method for encouraging empowerment within a team or organization.

9. Change is driven by inspiration or crisis. One leads to proactive, whole-brained thinking. The other is reactive and stems from the limbic brain. Fight or flight are high on its menu of options.

## CHAPTER TWELVE INSIGHTS

| SURVIVING | THRIVING |
| --- | --- |
| Assuming that someone can empower you or that you or someone else can actually "empower" another person. | Realizing that empowerment is a personal decision to perform at one's highest potential (it cannot be granted by another). |
| Delegating authority without making a proper assessment as to the clarity of the assignment, and the scope of authority within which a person must operate. | Properly assessing prospects for new assignments or advancement, ensuring that the assignment, scope of authority, and reporting timelines are clear and agreed upon. |
| Making assignments, particularly those that require a stretch, without proper support, coaching or mentoring. | Providing all of the necessary support and structure to enhance the opportunity for a person to empower themselves. |
| "Empowering" another person without properly determining their capability in terms of cognitive, interpersonal, and technical skills. | Ensuring cognitive, technical, and interpersonal skills are taken into account and coached and mentored where necessary. |

# PART FIVE

## Flipping the Script

*Where you reinvent the story
of your organization and your life
and learn what motivates you
to sustainable success.*

# Chapter Thirteen:

# Reclaiming Authorship of Your Own Story

*The most important question
anyone can ask is:
What myth am I living?*

~ Carl Jung

I (Chris) am sitting on a plane and I'm fuming. We've been on the tarmac for more than 20 minutes, waiting for our gate. The passenger next to me leans over and asks a seemingly innocent question. "How are you?" he says with a mischievous grin.

"Fine," I say gruffly. He doesn't buy it.

After he prods a bit I launch into a story about how my boss is clueless. He's sent me on this fool's errand to New York to deal with a customer he knows is impossible. He's put me on probation for insubordination. "He's setting me up," I tell my new friend.

It feels good to share my frustration with a total stranger.

"Are you OK with all that?" he asks with a wry smile. "Because if you are, just keep going with that same story and you'll get fired."

My jaw drops. Who is this guy?

He's just alerted me to a vicious program running in my mind that is poised to sabotage me without my even knowing it. Let's dig into this.

## WHAT IF I DON'T LIKE MY STORY?

In earlier chapters, we explored our natural and remarkable ability to create stories and then live them out as the primary protagonist, casting others in supporting roles.

We also highlighted the brain's propensity for using bias shortcuts, practical in some ways but also capable of leading us into brain blindness where we filter our experience to confirm our current version of reality.

Here are some bullet points and a diagram to clarify and detail what happens. Keep in mind what I told this stranger on the plane.

- We create a *story* (infused with meaning).

- The story casts a spell on our mind (i.e., we believe it's *the truth*).

- We assume a *role* based on that story and identify with it.

- This creates the filter through which we see the world and the *attitude* with which we approach people and situations.

- This state of mind then leads to *behaviors* (actions or inactions).

- This generates an *outcome* or *result* with short- and long-term implications.

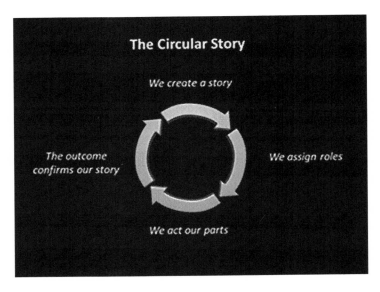

**The Circular Story**

*We create a story*

*We assign roles*

*We act our parts*

*The outcome confirms our story*

Outcomes are largely predetermined by the stories we create (which are almost always generated at an unconscious level). If we're satisfied with our outcome (achieved or anticipated), then nothing needs to change.

As this stranger told me, "Just keep going with that same story and you'll get fired."

Truth is, we often *don't* like our story. Certainly, if we become aware of undesirable consequences, we will be more inclined to wake up to what's happening. Of course, we don't always have a wise guy sitting beside us to help break the spell of disempowerment.

**THE DRAMA TRIANGLE**

Unless we're consciously aware of what we're doing, most of us are prone to create stories that generate dramas based on a familiar archetypal formula. Playwrights and philosophers identified this process eons ago, gave it various names, and have been using it ever since.

We use one of those names: The Drama Triangle.

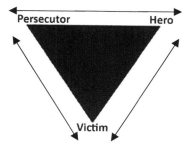

Some call this the Conflict Triangle or the Karpman Drama Triangle (after its inventor, Dr. Stephen Karpman, who studied under Dr. Eric Berne, the father of Transactional Analysis).

According to Karpman's theory, "Initially, a drama triangle arises when a person takes on the role of a victim, rescuer or persecutor. This person then feels the need to enlist other players into the conflict. These enlisted players take on roles of their own that are not static, which means that the scenario can shift.

"For example, a victim might turn on her rescuer, the rescuer could then switch to persecuting, or they could all support each other to identify as victims.

"The motivations for each participant and the reason the situation endures is that each gets their unspoken (and frequently unconscious) wishes/needs met in a manner they feel justified, without having to acknowledge the broader dysfunction or harm done in the situation as a whole. As such, each participant is acting upon their own selfish needs, rather than acting in a genuinely responsible or altruistic manner"[1]

Does this sound familiar to you?

Have you ever seen this play out in any of your true-life dramas? Perhaps you've witnessed it in the lives of your friends, family, or colleagues? And how about on a screen somewhere, on the public stage?

Politics, sports, entertainment, pretty much everything we create is based on interaction between these three components. There are victims (citizens, the downtrodden, a spurned lover). There are persecutors (government, big business, the competition). And there are rescuers (candidates, whistle blowers, co-dependent friends).

I (Will) was once hired to advise the director of a small nonprofit where conflict had escalated around an allegation of financial impropriety. Although these claims were quickly proven untrue, with appropriate legal documentation from attorneys and CPAs to prove it, the gossip continued, now centered on behaviors of the director.

During a mediation session, it became obvious that several on the leadership team were thoroughly entranced into victim roles.

The villain was obvious to them—their leader!

And the rescuer? That was the main gossip monger. Volunteers began jumping ship, even forming an alternate organization. It was a hopeless situation, as long as those involved continued to identify the way they did.

I'd like to say that it ended well but not every story has a Disney ending. The jury is still out on the final outcome as of this writing.

In order for the Drama Triangle to stay in place like this, all the players have to do is keep identifying themselves in one or more of these rotating roles, while casting others in their complimentary parts.

Of course, any of the participants can step outside the triangle and free themselves from the drama at any time by doing one simple thing—taking 100% responsibility for their participation in the situation.

This three-ring circus is constantly playing out in our lives and all around us. It's the foundation the status quo is built on. It's what marketing depends on and it's how politicians get elected.

If you're not seeing this pattern, you're either not paying attention or you're in a profound state of denial. Even the most responsible person can inadvertently fall into one of these roles, especially when someone puts out a casting call for the part and your past history (operated by your subconscious mind) responds without you even realizing it. "Pick me, I have experience!"

It's a slippery slope from that moment on.

After witnessing so many dramas play out in the film, television, and music industries, the entertainment company I (Chris) helped run adopted a mantra to live by: "Leave the drama on the screen."

## CREATING A NEW STORY

If you've come to a point where you'd like to step out of the Drama Triangle you've been part of or you'd like to upgrade your story and improve potential outcomes, we've got good news for you.

You've come to the right place. And, it's simple.

Simple, but not necessarily easy.

First, install a new story. Put your conscious mind in charge of a story upgrade. In other words, quit letting the dog drive the car just because he wants to be helpful. The dog is your unconscious, bias- driven mind.

Now, before we totally lose your attention to the visual of a dog driving your car, there's one important distinction we want to point out. This relates to the difference between first order change (merely changing your behavior) and second order change (transforming how you see and approach the situation).

This model was originally introduced to me (Chris) by Dr. William Guillory, my fellow passenger on the plane flight I mentioned at the beginning of this chapter. (Yes, that's who the guy was—the renowned laser chemist and leader in the science of consciousness and corporate transformation who became my lifelong friend and mentor.)

He schooled me in a very straightforward process.

1. When we imagine a new, truly transformative story—one that may prove our initial story wrong or incomplete—we generate a mental state that's open to new possibilities.

2. This leads us to explore different behaviors (ones we may have never even had access to in our previous state of mind) that in turn will lead to more productive outcomes.

3. Or you can reverse the process. Focus on the result you want, behave accordingly, and watch as your mindset adjusts to the new experience you're creating.

It's that simple. Of course, we also need to do it, not just think about it!

## ENSURING SUCCESS

While the concept and process are simple, the application is not always easy. In fact, we've found through our years of consulting and coaching that few people can fully implement new stories into their day-to-day life without co-conspirators.

That's why we recommend that clients pair up with a trusted friend, colleague, or family member who is willing to be their acting coach and accountability partner.

Your acting coach can help you stay in character relative to the new story you are living and make sure you don't slip back into that old role, the one that generated the old outcomes you no longer want or need.

This perfectly describes employing the principle of accountability we introduced earlier.

To ground this process for you, pick something from your personal or business life that you need help with and ask yourself these five questions:

1. What result do I truly want or need?

2. What role will I need to assume in the story I'm about to act out that will lead to that new result? Remember that one of the most effective roles you can take on is one where you try to prove your previously bias-laden story about the person or situation wrong (or at least discover that it's not the full story).

3. What attitude will I need to maintain to convincingly and authentically play my new role?

4. How will I show up? What will I say and do (or not say and not do) that is consistent with this new role and my new story?

5. How will I hold myself more powerfully accountable (acknowledging progress and catching myself when I slip back into an old less productive role)?

Write some notes and hang onto them. We'll walk you through a more imaginative process for installing the new story momentarily. This is where that trusted friend or colleague comes in.

Having your own personal acting coach/accountability partner who will check in with you to see how you're doing (more frequently at first, then less often as you embody your new role) makes a big difference. It's optimal, but not a necessity, if this person can witness your performance in person, to provide feedback along the way.

## FLIPPING THE SCRIPT

If you don't allow your conscious self—the part of you that's present and aware of your current circumstances—to take charge as the writer and director of your life movie, your unconscious mind will continue to run the show.

That ends up creating far more drama and trauma than is necessary or helpful because what's running your show is outdated, irrelevant programming.

At the beginning of this chapter we offered to show you a proven method (proven through decades of research and application) to generate more powerful results in your life, the kind of results you say you want and need,

Here it is, in two stages. First, it's about what's been happening until now that is in need of a positive change. You'll want to keep this simple, to avoid getting sucked back into the drama.

Stage One—Identify the Current Story

1.  Describe the current result or outcome.

2.  Identify the role you have been playing.

3.  Determine what attitude you've been fostering.

4.  Calculate how long you've been showing up this way.

5.  Determine how well you have been holding yourself accountable.

In step two, you'll need to engage your imagination.

Stage Two--Create the New Story

1.   What new result do you want or need? Envision the outcome as if it's already occurred. See yourself as successful. Use your imagination. Where are you? What are you wearing? Who else is there? What are you feeling?

2.   What role have you taken on in the new story that has led to that new outcome?

3.   What does it feel like to have let go of the old, counterproductive role? What new freedom and insight do you have from this new perspective?

4.   What attitude are you emulating that allows you to play the new role convincingly and authentically?

5.   How are people responding to your new attitude?

6.   How is it allowing you to tap into more possibilities and more of your genius?

7.   How are you showing up? What do you say and do (or not say and not do) that is consistent with your new role, story, and outcome?

8.   How are you holding yourself more accountable (acknowledging progress and catching yourself when you do it right and when you slip back into an old less productive role)?

9.   Who's helping you? How are you playing a similar role for them?

10.  What can you do today to put this new story and your new role into motion?

As you see, we're applying the power of "vision first, results now" to our process of Flipping the Script. In so doing, we are engaging the power of our subconscious mind.

Flipping the Script means that the more we envision and experience what we want, as a done deal, our reticular activating system will begin to sort your day-to-day experience for aspects of reality that affirm and help us create that outcome.

Here's an important tip: don't take yourself, or this process, too seriously!

We talked about having fun; this process can be and should be, entertaining! Hold it all lightly and be willing to laugh about your own foibles and mistakes along the way. Think of that word mistake (miss take). What movie do you think has ever been produced where the actors and director got it perfect on the first take every single time?

It's never happened.

It likely never will, because course correction is part of the navigation process in life. We try something, learn what worked and what didn't work, and we adjust accordingly.

By the way, it's easier to course correct once you're underway than to micro-manage aiming in the perfect direction before you even begin. If you've ever tried turning the steering wheel on your car while you are standing still you know what we mean.

Get moving first, then change direction. That's easier.

Remember, if you're consistently tense and frustrated, being hard on yourself or others, then you're operating primarily from the fight, flight, freeze, or faint part of your brain. It's there for a reason, to rescue you from imminent danger, but that may not be what's really needed in the moment.

Flipping your script means losing the tendency to dwell on what's wrong and getting stressed out . . . by having fun instead. Laughing at your own slip ups and keeping things buoyant will light your brain up. And it will certainly be appealing to those you're working or living with!

Plus, whenever we're having fun, we increase access to our imagination and improve our chances of downloading some real genius moments.

Who knew that facing challenges and managing change could be fun? The more you practice and play with this process, the easier it will become. Soon, you'll find that Flipping the Script is a natural part of your thriving experience.

As you will also discover, you don't need to wait for major events or dramas to engage this process. You can employ our visioning techniques to Flip the Script about a meeting you're about to walk into, for a trip you're nervous about, or to prepare for joining a new friend for dinner.

In the process of "Flipping the Script" you may also find—as The Empowerment Dynamic group (TED) suggests—that, as you  step outside the Drama Triangle, you begin to see yourself in the "Creator" role (rather than Victim), with others playing the roles of "Challenger" (instead of Persecutor), and "Coach" (instead of Hero).[2]

Remember, it's your story.  So write it and live it in a way that is aligned with your deepest values and in a manner that moves you forward towards what you truly want.

## CHAPTER THIRTEEN INSIGHTS

| SURVIVING | THRIVING |
|---|---|
| Holding on to your current role in the Drama Triangle as if it's your only option, regardless of the cost to you and others. | Creating a new role for yourself that allows a healthier mindset that can lead to more productive possibilities and outcomes. |
| Finding people who commiserate with you and with whom you can form a coalition to support your "need to be right." | Seeking people who will coach you to see more effective ways of approaching situations you find challenging so that clarity and fresh, innovative solutions open up. |
| Refusing to realistically seek a new more productive outcome, while being unwilling to hold yourself accountable for any meaningful change. | Flipping the Script by creating a new plan of action that leads to a more productive outcome, while including others in your process who will help you hold yourself accountable to make meaningful changes. |

# Chapter Fourteen:

# Motivation

*When things get tough, really tough,*
*your business will fail if you*
*don't have a deep sense*
*of purpose tied to it.*
*Without a clear reason to stick it out,*
*it's just too easy to walk away.*

~ Scott Duffy, from *Launch*

"What's the secret to success?"

That's what a student is said to have asked Socrates, centuries ago. Instead of answering, Socrates guided his young student down to the river. They waded in together and when the water reached up to their necks, Socrates dunked him and held his head down.

The student struggled frantically, finally managing to break free. He gasped for air, confused and angry.

Socrates smiled and said, "When you want success as much as you wanted air, you will achieve it."

## SIX FAILURES THAT TURNED AROUND[1]

1.  Arianna Huffington

    Before the heady days of Huffington Post, Huffington's second book was rejected 36 times before being published.

2.  Bill Gates

    His first company, Traf-O-Data, was a complete disaster.

3.  George Steinbrenner

Steinbrenner (owner of the New York Yankees) owned a small basketball team in 1960. The entire franchise went bankrupt.

4. Walt Disney

   Disney's first animation company, Laugh-O-Gram Films, was forced to close.

5. Steve Jobs

   Jobs was fired by Apple's board of directors.

6. Milton Hershey

   Hershey's first three candy-related ventures all failed.

## WHAT KEEPS YOU MOTIVATED?

There are thousands about stories of failures like these. How did these folks turn failure into success? Having a deep sense of purpose, as Scott Duffy mentioned in this chapter's opening quote, was essential, we're sure.

But that's not always enough. All of these leaders, and scores of others, were motivated by their own compelling visions. They wanted something strongly enough that they were able to navigate serious challenges and turn failure into success.

## PUSH OR PULL?

What keeps your vision compelling enough to motivate you through the inevitable white water that shows up on the journey from failure to success?

Experiencing the rewards of your success right now.

We wrote about this earlier when we studied the Titanic disaster. We'd like to go deeper now.

The secret is to be pulled towards your goals by a compelling vision. That's thriving. Without a compelling vision, the best you can do is push forward with brute strength. That's surviving.

Your vision has no such limits.

Take your pick: being pulled by a vision or pushing towards a goal.

When your vision becomes so real that you experience it *as if your goal is already achieved*, you will stay motivated.

As one of our well-practiced clients once shared, "Once you experience your vision as real, you feel like you're participating in its unfoldment, rather than wondering if it's going to happen."

## HELP ALONG THE TRAIL

I (Will) was backpacking with my wife and another couple in the Marble Mountains of Northern California, up around 5,000 feet. It was 90 degrees, I was lugging a heavy pack, and we were toiling uphill.

I engaged my vision as I hiked, imagining myself floating in Summit Lake (our destination), gazing up at the blue sky, hearing bird song, and feeling a gentle wind ripple the surface of the cool water.

Because I've practiced this so much, it was easy to incorporate the imaginary experience of swimming into my hiking. I still felt hot and fatigued but I simultaneously felt exhilarated by those sensations.

Every step on the trail became a stroke in the water.

## THE SLINKY EFFECT

Yes, it feels good to achieve whatever goal you set for yourself. But with our "vision first, results now" model you're not waiting for enjoyment; you're proactively creating it for yourself right now.

We call this The Slinky Effect, after that toy invented back in the '40s. You might remember setting one on the stairs and watching it loop its way down, front first, with the rear catching up.

Your compelling vision is the front end; your actions are the back end. This image demonstrates the vital connection between vision and action. If you don't first start the front end of the Slinky down the stairs (vision) just fiddling with the rear end (taking action) makes progress erratic.

## HARNESSING THE ENERGY OF COMPLETION

Whenever we complete something, we simultaneously begin something else. Nature is efficient that way; there are always an abundance of seeds that show up at harvest time. The same principle applies to us. Men release 200 – 600 million sperm cells (a completion) that all race towards a single egg (to create a beginning).

Back to the trail. When we arrived at Summit Lake and I (Will) dove in, I experienced much more than the immediate refreshment of cool water. My vision met my experience and what we term "the energy of completion" surged through my entire being.

The experience of vision meeting experience always proves exhilarating and success is always a great ongoing motivator.

## ANOTHER REASON TO ENJOY "NOW"

There's another way to look at why we should learn to enjoy our results right now.

In his 1981 book, Critical Path, Buckminster Fuller articulated what he called The Law of Precession. "Precession is the effect of bodies in motion on other bodies in motion."

His succinct definition is filled out in an online article: "It (precession) operates at 90 degrees (right angle) from the force. For example, the sun's gravity causes us to orbit around it at right-angles to the gravitational pull.[2]

Here's more from Bucky himself: "The successful regeneration of life growth on our planet Earth is ecologically accomplished always and only as the precessional—right-angled—"side-effect" of the biological species' . . . preoccupations."

And, from the article: "For example, the honey bee enters a flower in search of nectar to make honey. Inadvertently, it collects pollen at right angles to its nectar-seeking efforts and goes on to pollinate other flowers. The bees' activity supports its own species and unintentionally, the flowers that feed it."

Of course, bee activity also supports us. What would humans eat without the food that grows because bees pollinate?

But that is not the primary purpose of bees. The exact same "precessional" impact is at work in our lives.

We have our goal and we head towards it, but along the way we create ripples from our actions. According to Bucky, a greater value always accrues from that activity than does from reaching our goal.

Yes, we establish our goals and we work towards them, being pulled by our compelling vision. But, at the same time, we are *already* generating an impact. And, as Bucky says, the *way* we are living will ultimately have more impact than reaching our goal, however significant it might be. This motivates us to be fully responsible and accountable, to be fully present and to enjoy now.

This also introduces us to a new term: deep time.

**DEEP TIME**

Linear time rules our fragmented world where most people are multi-tasking, texting while they eat, watching screens big and small, with emails coming and going . . . it sounds exhausting reciting these details from our modern high-tech three-ring circus reality!

That's all happening in linear time, marching horizontally from past through present into the future. And, there never seems to be enough time! Anyone who can stand in the midst of it all and remain fully present gets noticed . . . because it's so rare.

Their secret? They know how to hang out in deep time.

Deep time is vertical, traveling deep into the present moment where—as quantum physicists assure us—linear time simply doesn't exist. Past, present, and future coexist together in deep time.

When we are in deep time, fully present, we pay attention to everything. "Great leaders take the time to understand the needs of their employees, and work with them to develop their talents so they can move up within the company, as well as increase their capacity to contribute to the team." [3]

Linear time relates to doing. It's task-based, moving laterally from past through present into the future, getting things done. Deep time relates to being, dropping down from superficiality into depth. Deep time increases intimacy, emotional connection, and authentic communication.

Deep time is also where the greatest fulfillment is experienced. We've all touched it and, when we do, we want more of it. OK, it feels good, those moments of timelessness. But is it practical?

Think for a moment about the costs of attrition and rehiring, having to constantly train new staff, plus all the dysfunctional ripple affects you can't even track.

Think about your family life, the cost of a divorce, the anguish of children gone to the dark side. All these are symptoms of deep time deficit. There's insufficient depth, connection, or authentic communication to develop and sustain a healthy business and family life.

You can't increase linear time. You can increase deep time.

## THE WISDOM OF DEEP TIME

I (Chris) have the honor of being friends with a woman who has a well-developed sense of deep time. Moved by the plight of people in Swaziland (a small country in Southern Africa), my friend Sally traveled there to help communities that had been decimated by AIDS.

Their most urgent needs were food and shelter for the orphans and medical care for those infected to stop the disease from spreading further.

But Sally approached those needs in a very different way than many other volunteers and NGOs who had been attempting to "fix" the problem.

Instead of rushing to the rescue like some sort of Florence Nightingale, Sally spent time with the people and got to know who their leaders were. She sat with them and listened . . . and listened, then listened some more.

She exhibited an open-hearted willingness to be fully present, and hear enough to develop a truly effective approach. She involved the communities in their own rebuilding process.

Being in deep time with these communities enabled Sally to fully understand what was *truly* needed and how to partner with villagers to create more sustainable solutions.

The wisdom she gained during deep time with those villagers also allowed her to return home and share her compelling vision with friends.

Her local church decided to adopt one of those African communities. Six years later they are still very much in relationship with those Swazi families.

I visited Sally and her team in that beautiful country and learned something else about deep time. In that powerful space of real presence, relationships were growing authentically, deeply, and quickly.

I learned firsthand how shared trust and respect can be truly profound and how mutual learning and the exchange of intangible value occurs.

## ENTRAINMENT

For Sally and many others like her, miracles begin with the creation of a compelling vision . . . then acting on it, as she did.

When your vision is real for you and passionate, everyone wants what you've got. You're motivated, and you motivate others.

The principle of entrainment begins to happen, where you influence others through what the Heart Math Institute refers to as an attunement of heart and brainwave frequencies. It's literally measurable. When this occurs, everything gets easier.

This always starts with "me" but it works best when it's not *about* "me," but "we."

## EXPANDING OUR WEALTH PORTFOLIO

In our consumer culture, we are programmed to equate wealth with material possessions. By now, we know that not only does money *not* make us happy, the love of money can actually impoverish us.

The villagers Sally met were rich in other ways. They may have been poor by our standards but they were wealthy in terms of their community experience.

If wealth is more than money, which it is, we can expand our understanding of the word "portfolio." What might it include besides money and physical assets? Here are a just a few of our non- material assets in an expanded wealth portfolio.

- Love: giving and receiving freely, growing self-esteem and faith in generosity.

- Friendship: deepening friendships and investing in long-term relationships.

- Health: making wellbeing our top priority, knowing that our investment in health is a wise one.

- Contribution: proactively developing our contributions within our communities.

If, instead of only counting money and stuff, we count these and other non-material assets, it becomes obvious that while money is an important part of our portfolio, it is not the only measurement of true wealth.

When we are motivated to achieve the expanded version of success we have been describing, we put money in its place and develop true wealth.

## THERE'S ALWAYS MORE

We wrote earlier about the Titanic Problem and identified that 87% of the average iceberg is hidden underwater. It's wise to remember that this principle is also true for everything in our personal and work lives.

For instance, we've just looked at wealth and seen more to it than money. How many other areas of our lives are ripe for re-visioning?

There's a reason why we don't see everything. It would be overwhelming. As we explored in an earlier chapter, we're bombarded with information 24/7. We see what we need to see, when we need to see it, until there's a reason to see more.

"With this onslaught of input, how do we manage to not go completely insane? The key is that we pay attention to only a small portion of that information and throw much of it away.

"This process is known as selective filtering or selective attention, and most people do it all the time. Imagine watching a movie at a theater. If you're quite focused on the film, you're probably not noticing the sound of squeaking seats, crunchy popcorn, or even the air conditioning whirring through the vents.[3]

What determines the kind of selective filtering that we do? Whatever is motivating us. When we're in the theater to watch a movie that's what we filter for. And we filter out peripheral noises; it's as if they aren't happening because they're not important in that moment.

I (Will) lived near the Vancouver, Canada airport during my twenties. Jets flew directly over our house and they were loud! After a few months, we stopped hearing them. I only realized this when I listened to a tape recording someone made of a class delivered in our home.

The speaker's voice was obliterated three or four times when a 747 flew overhead. I hadn't heard it. Later that year, air traffic controllers went on strike and we had a couple of days of silence. None of us in the house could sleep!

There is *always* more hidden than seen. It's not a possibility, it's a certainty. Knowing that we are going to filter, that it's the way our brains work, we can make the process more conscious and decide *what* we want to filter for.

Most of us have experienced what we call The Subaru Effect. If you shop for one, you start to see them everywhere. You are filtering *for* Subarus and there they are.

We also filter *out* information that we've determined—for whatever reason—we believe we don't need. We wrote about this before. Not seeing your keys on the table (because you filtered out that possibility, since you never put the keys there).

Developing deep time perception means challenging our unconscious filtering, making it more conscious. This makes us much more likely to anticipate the unseen in time to take corrective action.

Most important, incorporating this as part of our strategy motivates us to *want* to look. If we remain unconscious, we leave ourselves to the mercy of our programming and we *will* miss important information. If we become conscious about seeing more, we will.

## A NEW COMPASS

Living vision first, results now is like having a new kind of compass. It guides *and* motivates you. You can reference it any time, especially when you're faced with a decision. "Which path will grow the feeling I'm already having and lead me closer to my goal?"

This is not to suggest opting for comfort in the face of challenge. Quite the opposite. Having this perspective empowers you to do the hard work, because you're motivated, *not by the promise of future rewards but by the experience you're already having*. It feels good and you want more of that.

When you cross the finish line you get a bonus: the energy of completion. But you're not waiting for it. You're no longer in a world of hoped-for future rewards (what we refer to as "lottery consciousness"), you discover that fulfillment is always available now, well before you reach your goal.

When you master this principle, and are able to use it to motivate others, you'll find that no arm twisting is required to create stakeholders and loving friendships.

Who wouldn't want a piece of *that* action?

Something relaxing happens as you release your grip on the results you want later, because you're experiencing fulfillment now. Since you already have it, emotionally, you let go of any obsession you may have with your target vision and open to other possibilities.

You are filtering for that goal and others are helping, like your boss who makes it clear what *he* wants (allowing you to see if your own vision coincides). And your friend who is always whispering encouraging words in your ear.

All of us also carry programming we picked up from our parents. Sadly, many children live out their parents' dreams instead of their own. They are filtering out what *they* want in favor of what *dad* wanted for them (to fill some void in himself).

Put *your* vision first and experience the feeling of the results now. It's a far better compass.

## SPACE

I (Will) remember watching a TV interview program where the guest verbally attacked the host. He went on and on. I was appalled and then intrigued to see how the host would respond.

I've conducted hundreds of interviews myself and was busy thinking up my own strategies.

What he did surprised me.

When the guest finally ran out of steam the interviewer looked directly into the camera and said, "We need to take a commercial break; we'll be right back."

When they returned, he asked a new question. He didn't defend himself. In fact, he didn't respond to the tirade at all. I remember the guest looking sheepish and imagined that, during the break, he realized that he may have lost it. Perhaps he was even grateful the host didn't challenge him back.

Space.

Space can work wonders. The interviewer created space; he took a break. Sometimes that's the best strategy for us, especially when we're feeling the urge to act.

How many disastrous tweets would never have been sent if someone had paused before clicking SEND, if they had created space to let their emotions settle down?

There are countless examples of this space principle in action. An inventor is struggling with his experiments. He goes for a walk, let's go of his frustration, and comes up with a brilliant answer . . . for a completely different invention.

Dynamite was discovered that way, as we mentioned, so was the pacemaker, Post-It Notes, Super Glue, Teflon, and . . . the Slinky![4]

Our best motivation is provided by a compelling vision that enables us to face the facts of the situation, leverage available resources, look beneath the surface, consciously manage our filtering, and create the space we need to gain perspective.

All of that can create the success and happiness we want, a truly thriving experience.

## CHAPTER FOURTEEN INSIGHTS

| SURVIVING | THRIVING |
|---|---|
| Pushing towards goals that are disconnected from a compelling vision. | Being pulled towards goals by a compelling vision. |
| Ignoring the significance of a small success. Make up what comes next, disconnected from what you just completed. | Celebrating each milestone of accomplishment and harvesting the energy of completion. |
| Failing to connect cause and effect. | Employing "The Slinky Effect." |
| Overemphasizing the value of accomplishing one goal. | Working with "The Law of Precession." |
| Operating solely in linear time, while only focusing on quantitative outcomes. | Operating in deep time and focusing on both quantitative *and* qualitative outcomes. |

# PART SIX

# Implementation

*Where we summarize
and apply our principles for thriving
to regenerate your life and work.*

# Chapter Fifteen:

# Thriving at Work

*"Being a great place to work
is the difference between being
a good company and a great company."*

~Brain Kristofek

Kathryn approached her CEO a few months after being hired. He'd always made himself available to the staff regardless of a busy schedule laced with international travel.

"Do you have a moment?" she asked him.

"Certainly, Kathryn . . . what is it? the CEO asked.

"You know how, during the interview process, you said that the culture here was the key to our success?" Kathryn began. "That being here for each other and having each other's backs was essential?"

"I do remember that," the CEO responded.

"I was hesitant to believe that," Kathryn confessed. "Don't get me wrong. I wanted to believe it. But in this industry, it seemed impossible and yet, it's true here. How did you do that?"

"I didn't," the CEO responded. "We all did it together. And we continue doing it each day by the way we act and how we hold ourselves and each other accountable."

**WHO ARE YOU TO MAKE A DIFFERENCE?**

You may not be the CEO of a company. You may not be in any formal position of authority. But regardless of your position, you *are* a leader. The question is, where are you leading? What are you modeling? What story are you creating? What vision are you bringing to life each day?

One of the biggest con jobs we can fall for is believing we can't make a difference. That the world, our industry, our company, or department, has all the control.

Do those larger entities have some control? Absolutely! And so do we. How?

We decide every day, and in every moment, how we will respond to what comes our way.

The humanitarian Albert Schweitzer said it this way. "You may not be able to change the whole world. But you can change the world for one person, if you try."

The first person that may apply to is you. After you've removed the log from your eye, you can help others remove the speck from theirs, as the saying goes.

While engaged at work, we are constantly challenged with many tasks and goals. We also interact with people—living, breathing human beings—every day. The attitude we lead with, the energy we express, our very way of being, impacts the people and collective culture around us.

I (Chris) remember my first real job after college. I was working as a sales representative for a trucking company and, as one of the newly hired employees, I was offered a mentor—Kelly—a recently retired sales rep who'd achieved legendary success.

All the new hires were offered this opportunity but I was the only one who accepted it. "I don't need some old guy going on and on about the way things used to be," one of my colleagues said, justifying his decision to pass on the opportunity.

Over the next six months, Kelly took me under his wing and showed me things that I've never forgotten. For instance, he told me, "The main secret to selling is to stop selling."

"Be with people," he continued. "Ask them how they're doing and then listen. Show them you care. Find out what they really need and if you can fill that need, then do it with class and distinction."

"And if I can't?" I asked.

"Then connect them with someone who can," he answered quickly.

"Even if it's the competition?" I challenged.

"You don't have any competition other than yourself," Kelly said with a chuckle. "Trust me. If you learn to love the people you serve and treat them with the type of care they need, you'll have more of their business than you can handle."

I nodded, having seen how beloved he was by his own customers.

"That so-called competition," Kelly said with a wink, "will become your collaborators. Then you can serve all your customers, together."

That type of attitude had served Kelly and his customers marvelously well. It was obvious that Kelly knew how to thrive and, as a result, everyone around him had a better chance to thrive as well.

Many years later, I attended Kelly's funeral. The church house overflowed with family and friends, customers and competition. The eulogies were as varied as the people, but they all had one theme in common. Kelly was honored as a simple man who had made an extraordinary difference in the lives of hundreds and hundreds of people, while carrying out his very ordinary eight-hour-a-day job.

**SEIZING THE OPPORTUNITY**

Work throws us into the midst of people and situations we would never otherwise experience. What will we choose to do with those remarkable opportunities, with the diversity of people, personalities, and experiences we're provided with?

If we choose to thrive at work, encounters with outliers from our primary peer group will become enlivening and challenges will invigorate us.

If we choose to merely survive, work will remain or become a drudgery, increasingly difficult to tolerate.

Thriving at work is certainly simpler if our organizational culture encourages it and if our managers and leaders personally and proactively support it. But our choice to survive or thrive is not up to them. It's not up to anyone else, for that matter. It's up to each of us to decide for ourselves.

Lest we think our decision is merely a personal one, let's remember the profound ripple effect we have on those around us. Our actions, our words, and our attitudes affect everyone.

As coaches, we hear stories regularly about how one person lit up their entire team. We all have that exponential power and influence at our disposal, if we choose to use it.

Stand upstream as you prepare to begin each workday and ask: "What's my vision for today? What story will I create in the next eight to ten hours? Who will I impact and what impact will I let allow others to have on me?

We know one thing is sure: Thriving is more fun than surviving! It's far healthier too, for you and everyone around you. And, it's a better pathway to success.

Why not go for it? Muster the courage to thrive. See how many others you can enroll to join your conspiracy to rejuvenate your workplace. Ask for help when you need it.

We have one life to live. Make it count. Make that meeting you're about to walk into brighter, more alive, more focused, more human because you're there. Turn the difficult conversation you're dreading into an opportunity to model compassion and deep understanding.

As we seize the moments, we discover that life-giving actions are contagious. You may even find yourself committing random acts of kindness towards those who have previously bothered you the most.

In the end, love and compassion are infectious in the best of ways. They foster genius—in you and in others—genius we need now and in the challenging years ahead.

We may think we work for an organization and we may. But we also work in the world and when we thrive at work we contribute to more thriving in the world. Thriving at home is vital as well, and we'll address that in the next chapter, but work usually gives us more diverse opportunities for influence.

How many people—fellow employees, managers, customers—can we infect with the thriving virus? They say that smiles are infectious; so are attitudes. People who knew Steve Jobs said that he had a powerful "reality warp field," referring to his energy and how it influenced them. We all have a field of influence, in us and extending beyond us. When we are thriving, anyone who comes near us can be entrained and inspired into thriving in their own way. What better contribution can we make?

And, if you don't believe that our energy and attitude affect the bottom line, just study the companies that continue to be successful year after year. You'll usually find that they consciously maintain a thriving culture.

**CHAPTER FIFTEEN INSIGHTS**

| SURVIVING | THRIVING |
|---|---|
| Expecting other people to hold themselves accountable while letting yourself off the hook. | Owning your decisions and their impact. You make the difference. |
| Controlling others from a safe emotional distance. | Being truly present with people. |
| Sleep walking through your life and your work. | Seizing every opportunity to generate excellent high-quality work and interactions. |

# Chapter Sixteen:

# Thriving in Life

*"Do you want to be in your own story*
*or on the outside writing about it?*
*Everyone battles fear and uncertainty every day.*
*However, the only failure in life is believing that your value*
*relies on other people's approval or resources.*

*"The reality is this: When you are living your authentic self*
*and not how people want you to act,*
*then you are free to use the full spectrum*
*of your creativity and gifts.*

*"People don't need resources to get out of any life situation.*
*They need creativity to create resources.*
*When you realize that, becoming stuck is impossible."*

~ Shannon L. Alder

After 21 years of marriage, Fred's wife suggested he take another woman out to dinner—his mother.

He called to invite her and, after inquiring if he was OK, his mother said, "I would like that very much."

At the restaurant, Fred had to read the menu to his mother whose eyesight was failing. She remarked, "I used to read the menu to you when you were small," she said.

"Well then, let me return the favor," Fred responded.

They enjoyed a wonderful dinner, sharing family memories in a way they never had.

A few days later, Fred's mother died of a massive heart attack. The next week, he received an envelope in the mail with a copy of a restaurant receipt from the same place they had dined.

An attached note said: "I paid this bill in advance because I wasn't sure that I would be there. I paid for two plates—one for you and the other for your wife. You will never know what that night meant for me. I love you, son." [1]

## INVESTING LOVE IN OUR FAMILIES

If you haven't lost a close family member yet, you will. Some of them will lose you. The anguish of losing those we love the most is the price we pay for loving so deeply.

I (Will) was with my mother during the last three days of her life and listened to her speak with regret about the opportunities she'd missed for sharing more with her three daughters-in-law.

"Why did I work so hard?" she wondered. "Why didn't I have more fun with the girls?"

No one comes to the end of their life and wishes they'd spent more time in the office. No, we miss the love we missed.

I remember overhearing a close friend talking with his two young sons one night. The conversation went something like this: "Is there anything we need to talk over from today, guys?"

"No, Dad," one of his sons said.

My friend offered, "Well, there's something I need to say. I want to apologize for getting impatient when we were working on the bike."

His boys assured him it was OK, but I could tell they appreciated his honesty. They continued to talk about that incident and then a few others that had occurred that day.

Now, a decade later, those lads are young adults and I witness how they treat others with the same respect and consideration they exchanged with their father that night. One of the boys got married recently to an honest, loving person, just like him.

My friend's investment in love has paid off big time. His family is thriving.

## LITTLE THINGS COUNT

Little things count towards big results. Moments like those my friend spent with his sons were symptomatic of life in their family: honest and real, with time to talk over problems openly.

A thriving personal life develops because we make it a priority and invest the necessary time. Doing that sets a tone for the kind of people we end up attracting into our lives, beyond our blood families.

I (Will) will never forget waiting for my wife to get out of surgery. I kept leaving the family room where I was waiting to stare down the long hallway towards the double doors she had been wheeled through, long hours before.

Suddenly, I heard them open.

I rushed out and there was the surgeon, heading towards me. The moment she saw me she made a vigorous thumbs-up sign.

That's an example of the little things we're talking about.

She'd been there many times before. She knew how anxious I would be so she didn't wait to get closer to give me the good news. The moment our eyes met she made the all-clear sign.

I'll never forget her kindness.

For me (Chris), I'll always remember one moment during the week before my father unexpectedly passed away. My wife and I had taken him and my mother to breakfast at one of our favorite cafés. It happened to be next to a bookstore that we loved.

Following our meal, we browsed through the bookstore with my parents, who were both avid readers. As Dad and I ventured off to explore an aisle on world culture and spirituality, we paused at the section on India.

Dad had spent a number of years in India while in the military and had often regaled me with stories and shown me photos and souvenirs that he'd gathered from those days. For some reason, he'd stopped doing that after I grew up.

But on this occasion, he picked up a book on Indian culture and began to share stories about his time there, stories I'd never heard before. "I know you're intrigued by India," he said to me. "And I know that I shut you off the last few times you asked me about it," he confessed.

"You see," he went on, "I experienced a lot of pain there. I guess I was trying to shield you from that."

I started to thank him, but he stopped me.

"No," he said. "If we're going to be in an honest relationship then we can't be selective. We need to share the whole story so we can really understand each other. I want to do that."

And so he told more stories and I listened. It was wonderful.

Those moment of deep disclosure and the others like them that preceded his peaceful passing several nights later taught me lessons about authenticity, deep time, and the power of love that have served me my entire life. He let me "know him;" what a heartfelt gift from a father to his son.

## ENJOY YOUR LIFE

We salute you for the love you invest in your personal relationships and wish you our best to develop a thriving personal life.

As American author H. Jackson Brown, Jr., advised: "Live so that when your children think of fairness, caring, and integrity, they think of you."

Live so that everyone else thinks of you that way too.

That's the kind of personal leadership that develops a thriving world, one honest, caring relationship at a time.

## CHAPTER SIXTEEN INSIGHTS

| SURVIVING | THRIVING |
|---|---|
| Missing family life by staying in your head about work while at home. | Investing love in your family by giving them your full attention when you are with them. |
| Focusing on big challenges and missing small, important details. | Making sure that the little things count. |
| Compromising your own values to succeed. | Living your values fully as an integral part of success. |

# Chapter Seventeen:

# Live Your Dream

*"Life is a puzzle, a riddle, a test, a mystery, a game—*
*whatever challenge you wish to compare it to.*
*Just remember, you're not the only participant;*
*no one person holds all the answers,*
*the pieces, or the cards.*

*"The trick to success in this life*
*is to accumulate teammates and not opponents."*

~ Richelle E. Goodrich

JT Smith founded The Game Crafter so he could make games without needing to get them from China. He wrote a Web app to upload and proof his artwork. He was surprised when his website turned into a business. He started selling games and by 2013 was selling 3,000 games a month.[1]

Nicole Snow decided to combine her two life passions, art and helping others, to create her own business, Darn Good Yarn. She began working with small businesses in India and Nepal and now, five years later, employs 300 women in those countries.[2]

Christine Watanabe couldn't find a tennis scorekeeper so she invented her own. With the help of a plastics engineer she created Score At Hand, which now sells in stores and online.[3]

**DO WHAT YOU LOVE**

What do these three entrepreneurs have in common?

They all turned personal interests into thriving businesses. Their lesson for us? Do what you love.

We love helping individuals and organizations move from surviving to thriving. We've dedicated our lives to this and, trust us, it's more rewarding than retiring!

With this book, we're sharing our two lifetimes of experience, including the many important lessons we've learned, mainly, that it's no longer enough to balance work and life. The line between personal and professional is blurring and disappearing. There are good things about that and some problems.

## BE AT HOME

Taking your work home can be one of those problems. "Enough already" might be the silent protest from a spouse or your children. It's not that they're disinterested in your work, it's that they want to connect with you. They can't, if your head stays back in the office.

Their request? Be present.

We wrote about "situational awareness." As we near the end of our book, we want to emphasize this as a priority because it's a secret to thriving: be fully present to engage and enjoy. There's an intimacy to authentic connection and *that's* what we all want.

Your spouse and kids want that; your business colleagues want that. *You* want that.

Children might tell a parent, years down the road, "I didn't feel you were really there for me." It's one of the toughest messages you might ever receive. A supervisor might question an employee: "Are you 100% committed here?"

If you take away this one tip and apply it diligently you will stay on course along your journey from surviving to thriving.

Engage. Choose to be "here," even though here is where the challenges are. It's also the domain of opportunity.

## SUMMARY

We began by identifying the difference between facts and the stories we tell about them, to help you know how to tell (and create) a story of thriving in your organization and in your life.

We shared our secret sauce, a process for visioning the results you want and using that as a compass for navigating to sustainable success and happiness.

You studied how to shed bias and be more inclusive, to be honest in your assessment of the way things currently are, and how to ask for help from both available and hidden resources.

You learned about quantum responsibility and how to develop teams/families of 100% accountability.

We explained how to "flip the script" for your life and organization. Circumstances always include limitations but using our ability to focus intention, our imaginations, and our commitment to daily action, can turn those limitations into opportunities.

Implementing the principles and techniques we've presented and truly benefiting from their deeper value comes from following through, one insight at a time. We highly recommend the buddy system for support so you continue moving in the right direction and get the new results you envision.

**WHAT'S CALLING YOU?**

Ultimately, thriving is doing what you love. But we make an important distinction. Yes, find what you love and do that. But also, learn to love what you are doing.

I (Chris) mentioned how my father told me to ask myself what I'd love to do even if I didn't get paid for it and to make that my vocation. He helped me understand that—given how many hours I'd be spending at work—I'd better work at something I enjoyed.

I (WILL) learned to engage. My wife's serious health challenge forced me to confront habits of aloofness, to develop more empathy and compassion for others.

We were called to work together, consulting, mentoring, conducting trainings. We were called to write this book. What are *you* called to do?

**STAYING ON TRACK**

As we mentioned, planes are off course about 85% of the time. The pilot course corrects successfully because he knows his destination. He also knows his starting point.

A pilot expects to go off course and he knows how to correct. Life can be the same. Instead of getting frustrated when something throws us off track, we can deal with it from a position of confidence.

"This is what's supposed to happen" is very different from "Why is this happening?"

"Mission drift" is a term we wrote about briefly, described as the temptation to depart from your plan. We do recommend creating an image to symbolize your trajectory towards success. You can imagine one and think of it occasionally or you can find an actual visual and paste it on your wall. Having a reminder out there, just at the corner of your seeing, can be subliminally motivating.

## MAKE IT SO

We've presented a host of insights, skills, and guidance for implementation. Underneath the complexity lies a single truth: the difference between surviving and thriving is in our hands and it's called taking 100% responsibility. You now understand the power and nuances of this, and know that fully understanding this one concept, and acting on it, can transform both your life and your work.

As you complete this read, we invite you to make a commitment—to yourself. Is there anything more important than this? Your commitment to thriving will affect everyone in your life and everyone you work with. Most important, it will carry you from the mediocrity of making a living to the fulfillment of finding your calling . . . and fully embracing it.

Some of us have big missions, others toil in relative obscurity. Turns out that our public profile doesn't really matter that much. Each of us has a life and the value of it is only ever fully known to ourselves.

We know right now how fully we have embraced this life or not.
We'll know it as we breathe our last.

Why not seize this moment and commit to thriving? This book may be ending but there's a next chapter—the one you write for your life!

We'd love to hear from you about your stories of thriving. You can contact us via our website, www.thrivinginbusinessandlife.com where you'll also find additional resources and help.

*Until one is committed, there is hesitancy, the chance to draw back, always ineffectiveness. Concerning all acts of initiative (and creation), there is one elementary truth, the ignorance of which kills countless ideas and splendid plans: that the moment one commits oneself, then Providence moves too.*

*All sorts of things occur to help one that would never otherwise have occurred. A whole stream of events issues from the decision, raising in one's favor all manner of unforeseen incidents and meetings and material assistance, which no man could have dreamt would have come his way.*

*Whatever you can do, or dream you can, begin it. Boldness has genius, power, and magic in it!*

~ W. H. Murray

*There shall always be that voice that will tell you how you are wasting your time and ability, how you shall fail, how some tried and failed, why your prevailing slips are indications of your future doom, why you are unworthy to dare, why your background mismatches your vision and aspiration, why your personality misfits your mission and how arduous the errand is.*

*You have a choice. You have your thought. You have what burns in you that tells you how you can make it. Though the world may be interested in your success, it is much interested in your slips and mediocrity as well.*

*Your vision must keep you in your mission. Dare in wisdom. Dare unrelentingly. Ponder!*

~ Ernest Agyemang Yeboah

## ENDNOTES

### CHAPTER ONE

1. https://www.umass.edu/newsoffice/article/umass-amherst-researcher-finds-most-people-lie-everyday-conversation
2. http://shadhelmstetter.com/about-dr-helmstetter/
3. http://www.abouthypnosis.com/everyday-trance-states.html; http://pdhypnosis.com/our-unconscious-trance-states/

### CHAPTER TWO

1. Harvard Implicit Association Tests https://implicit.harvard.edu/implicit/takeatest.html
2. Malcolm Gladwell, *Blink – The Power of Thinking Without Thinking* (WestBow Press Publishing - A Division of Zondervan, 2005), 95

### CHAPTER THREE

1. Warren "Trapper" Woods and William A. Guillory, Ph.D, *Tick-Tock, Who Broke the Clock* (Innovations International, 2003)

### CHAPTER FOUR

1. Jim Dethmer, Diana Chapman, and Kaley Warner Klemp, *The 15 Commitments of Conscious Leadership: A New Paradigm for Sustainable Success* (Detmer, Chapman, & Klemp , 2015), 72
2. Robert Fritz, *The Path of Least Resistance* (Ballantine Books, 1984), 166
3. https://www.psychologytoday.com/blog/flourish/200912/seeing- is-believing-the-power-visualization
4. Ibid
5. https://en.wikipedia.org/wiki/Michael_Ovitz

### CHAPTER FIVE

No references

### CHAPTER SIX

1. Richard Bach, *Jonathan Livingstone Seagull* (MacMillan Publishers, 1970), 42
2. http://www.nbcnews.com/science/10-causes-titanic-tragedy-620220

3. Ibid
4. Ibid
5. http://www.cnet.com/news/titanic-disaster- unlikely-to-happen-in-this-age-experts-say/
6. Charles Dughigg, from *The Power of Habit*, (Random House, 2012), 178
7. http://www.geniusstuff.com/blog/list/10-accidental-inventions/


CHAPTER SEVEN

1. http://www.devicemagic.com/blog/kodak-moment
2. http://www.investopedia.com/financial-edge/0512/6-women-who-turned-failing-companies-into-a-success.aspx
3. Robert Fritz, *The Path of Least Resistance* (Ballantine Books, 1984), 145
4. Jim Dethmer, Diana Chapman, and Kaley Warner Klemp, *The 15 Commitments of Conscious Leadership* (Detmer, Chapman, & Klemp, 2015), 45
5. http://www.uua.org/re/tapestry/youth/call/workshop1/171686.s html


CHAPTER EIGHT

1. https://www.scientificamerican.com/article/how-diversity-makes-us-smarter/
2. https://provost.virginia.edu/sites/provost.virginia.edu/files/Making%20the%20Difference-Logic%20of%20Diversity_Page_Perspectives.pdf
3. Dr. Barbara Frederickson, *Love 2.0* (Penguin Publishing Group, 2013), 19

CHAPTER NINE

1. http://www.audubon.org/news/the-nature-conservancy-and-shell-oil-form-unlikely-partnership- save-important
2. Michael Pollan, *The Intelligent Plant* (The New Yorker, 2013)
3. https://en.wikipedia.org/wiki/Carl_Jung

4. http://www.smh.com.au/lifestyle/life/millions- of-men-have-no-close-friends-20151116- glo3cp.html
5. https://en.wikipedia.org/wiki/Lifeboats_of_the_RMS_Titanic

CHAPTER TEN AND ELEVEN

No references

CHAPTER TWELVE

1. William A. Guillory and Linda Galindo, *Empowerment for High Performing Organizations* (Innovations International, 1994)
2. Ken Blanchard, *Leadership and the One-Minute Manager* (Harper Collins, 2000)

CHAPTER THIRTEEN

1) Stephen Karpman, M.D, *The Drama Triangle,* https://en.wikipedia.org/wiki/Karpman drama triangle
2) TED (The Empowerment Dynamic) http://powerofted.com/the-ted-triangle/

CHAPTER FOURTEEN

1. https://www.entrepreneur.com/article/240492
2. http://davidya.ca/2013/02/28/making-a-living-through-precession/
3. https://www.psychologytoday.com/blog/brain-babble/201502/is-how-the-brain-filters-out-unimportant-details
4. http://www.nbcnews.com/id/38870091/ns/technology_and_science-innovation/t/greatest-accidental- inventions-all-time/

CHAPTER FIFTEEN

1. Edited from http://www.inspire21.com/stories/familystories/beingamother

CHAPTER SIXTEEN

1. http://mconideas.tumblr.com/post/96708544760/the-game-crafter-was-founded-in-2009-by-jt-smith
2. https://www.darngoodyarn.com/
3. https://www.youtube.com/watch?v=59A2l56ojHo

CHAPTER SEVENTEEN

1. http://mconideas.tumblr.com/post/96708544760/the-game-
   crafter-was-founded-in-2009-by-jt-smith
2. https://www.darngoodyarn.com/
3. https://www.youtube.com/watch?v=59A2l56ojHo
4. William Hutchison Murray (with a final couplet by Johann
   Wolfgang Goethe)

**Other Books by the Authors:**

Will Wilkinson

Perfect Health in a Perfect World
Attunement with Life
Forgiving the Unforgivable (collaboration)
Awakening from the American Dream (collaboration)
Living an Awakened Life - Lessons in Love (collaboration)
Now or Never

Christopher Harding

The Saint of Malibu Shores
The Future Perfect Organization (collaboration)
Spirituality in the Workplace (co-editor)
The Reindeer Boy
Messages in the Middle of the Night

Made in the USA
Middletown, DE
07 February 2019